THE JURY SYSTEM

Other Books in the At Issue Series:

Affirmative Action
Business Ethics
Domestic Violence
Environmental Justice
Ethnic Conflict
Immigration Policy
Legalizing Drugs
The Media and Politics
The Militia Movement
Policing the Police
Rape on Campus
Single-Parent Families
Smoking
The Spread of AIDS
The United Nations
U.S. Policy Toward China
Voting Behavior
Welfare Reform
What Is Sexual Harassment?

THE JURY SYSTEM

David Bender, *Publisher*
Bruno Leone, *Executive Editor*

Scott Barbour, *Managing Editor*
Brenda Stalcup, *Series Editor*

Mary E. Williams, *Book Editor*

An Opposing Viewpoints ® Series

Greenhaven Press, Inc.
San Diego, California

Library of Congress Cataloging-in-Publication Data

The jury system / Mary E. Williams, book editor.
    p.   cm. — (At issue)
    Includes bibliographical references and index.
    ISBN 1-56510-540-0 (lib. : alk. paper) — ISBN 1-56510-539-7
(pbk. : alk. paper)
    1. Jury—United States. I. Williams, Mary E., 1960-   . II. Series:
At issue (San Diego, Calif.)
KF8972.J878   1997
347.73'752—dc20
[347.307752]   96-41069
                                                                    CIP

© 1997 by Greenhaven Press, Inc., PO Box 289009,
San Diego, CA 92198-9009

Printed in the U.S.A.

Table of Contents

	Page
Introduction	6
1. The Jury System: An Overview *Kenneth Jost*	9
2. Trial by Jury Should Be Abolished *Christie Davies*	19
3. The Jury System Should Be Retained *Barbara Allen Babcock*	22
4. The Majority Verdict Should Be Adopted *Jacob Tanzer*	25
5. The Unanimous Verdict Should Be Retained *Jeffrey Abramson*	28
6. Peremptory Challenges Should Be Abolished *H. Lee Sarokin and G. Thomas Munsterman*	38
7. Peremptory Challenges Should Be Retained *Raymond Brown*	41
8. Juries Should Be Informed of Their Right to Nullify the Law *Larry Dodge*	51
9. Jury Nullification Should Not Be Allowed *Mark S. Pulliam*	59
10. Selected Racially Based Nullification Can Create Justice *Paul Butler*	63
11. Racially Based Jury Nullification Is Not Just *Michael Weiss and Karl Zinsmeister*	68
Organizations to Contact	74
Bibliography	76
Index	78

Introduction

On October 3, 1995, 150 million Americans watched the televised verdict of the criminal trial in which a jury found O.J. Simpson not guilty of murdering his ex-wife Nicole Simpson and her friend Ronald Goldman. For sixteen months, the public had been riveted by the high-profile trial—from revelations about Simpson's spouse abuse to confusion over DNA evidence to allegations of racism in the Los Angeles Police Department. Throughout the proceedings, the media had reported deep racial divisions in public opinion about Simpson: A majority of whites believed he was guilty and a majority of blacks believed he was innocent. When the not-guilty verdict was aired, many newscasts showed black observers cheering while white observers fumed in silence. This apparent difference of opinion was supported by statistics. According to a *Newsweek* poll, 85 percent of blacks agreed with the verdict while 54 percent of whites disagreed. A majority of those polled also believed that race had significantly influenced the verdict; many said they felt this way because most of the jurors were the same race as Simpson.

The Simpson trial was just one in a string of highly publicized trials with controversial verdicts that have focused public attention on the issue of jury-system reform. Critics of the not-guilty verdict in the Simpson trial, for example, raised concerns about the jury-selection process that had allowed a black defendant to be tried by a mostly black jury. A legal dispute arose over whether a juror could make an unbiased decision involving a defendant or a plaintiff of the same race, gender, religion, or socioeconomic class. This controversy had emerged before the Simpson trial: In 1992, an all-white jury acquitted four white police officers on charges of using excessive force in the beating of black motorist Rodney King; in 1991, an all-female jury in Alabama convicted James E. Bowman on paternity-suit charges.

The question of whether or not a jury should be balanced in terms of ethnicity, class, or gender is not new. In England, the jury's birthplace, the privilege of trial by a representative or "mixed" jury was allowed until the year 1290. At that time, a representative jury usually meant that half of the jurors were Christian and half of the jurors were Jewish. These mixed-jury trials generally served to protect the minority Jewish population; in other words, Jewish defendants who might face discrimination from an all-Christian jury fared better in mixed-jury trials. Eventually, however, the British adopted the custom of choosing a jury from the neighborhood in which the crime was committed. The U.S. Constitution retained this practice in its Sixth Amendment, which guarantees "the right to a speedy and public trial, by an impartial jury of the state and district wherein the crime shall have been committed." Thus, a "jury of peers" was originally a group chosen from the vicinity of the defendant's residence or from the area where the alleged crime occurred. Initially, there was no effort to include women or members of ethnic minorities on American juries. Ultimately, though, a jury of one's peers came to be defined as a group that reflected the country's racial, class, and gender composition. The contemporary practice of using voter-registration lists to create a jury pool is intended to ensure that minorities and women are included on juries.

Many twentieth-century legal analysts, however, have argued that additional efforts are needed to ensure that juries are balanced. Supporters of reinstituting the mixed-jury system contend that although using voting lists may produce a more diverse jury pool, it does not ensure that every jury will be diverse. American communities are often racially or socioeconomically isolated, they maintain, and juries chosen from such communities are likely to consist of members of just one race or socioeconomic class. Proponents of mixed juries argue that the modern definition of a jury of peers does not guarantee that minority plaintiffs or defendants will have minority jurors hear their case. Under the current system, critics maintain, people of color often fear that they will face discrimination from homogeneous, majority-group juries. According to a 1996 *Issues and Controversies on File* article, "Blacks, especially, have told pollsters that they do not trust all-white juries to deal with black defendants fairly." In response to arguments that mixed juries ensure minorities' right to a fair trial, several state legislatures have proposed laws requiring racially balanced juries.

Opponents of mixed juries, on the other hand, maintain that mistrials often occur when jury panels divide along racial or gender lines. This kind of split took place in the original 1994 trial of Erik Menendez, who, along with his brother Lyle, was accused of murdering his parents. In that trial, six male jurors voted for a murder conviction while six female jurors, accepting the defense's claim that Erik committed his crime because of years of parental abuse, chose the less severe manslaughter conviction. The result was a hung jury and a retrial. Many jury-system critics argue that such racially or sexually polarized settings can cause jurors to make unjust decisions based on emotion, prejudice, and preconception rather than on solid evidence. Therefore, these commentators conclude, mixed-jury trials do not necessarily guarantee that justice will be served.

For judges and lawyers, the question of the jury's composition is especially complex. Though lawyers do not actually choose the jurors who will hear their cases, they can eliminate prospective jurors by using "for cause" and "peremptory" challenges. During the jury-selection process, the judge and the opposing attorneys usually question potential jurors about their backgrounds, prior knowledge of the case, and opinions on relevant issues. Obviously biased candidates are immediately disqualified by "for cause" challenges; however, each side is also allowed up to twenty-five "peremptory" challenges, which enable lawyers to reject potential jurors without having to provide a reason. With these challenges, lawyers attempt to create a jury that will arrive at a decision favorable to their clients.

Most trial lawyers support the use of peremptory challenges, believing that they ensure impartial and representative juries. As Minneapolis attorney G. Marc Whitehead asserts, "Peremptories offer an opportunity for the litigators to exercise challenges that are not traditionally recognized by the law for cause but can eliminate people who are unwilling or unable to listen to one or both sides of a case." Many legal teams hire jury consultants to assist them in the jury-screening process, especially in high-profile cases. Jury consultants use some of the tools from commercial market research—polls, statistical profiles, interviews, questionnaires, handwriting analysis, mock juries—to help lawyers spot unsympathetic jurors. Before the O.J. Simpson trial, for example, the defense team's jury consultant Jo-Ellan Dimitrius surveyed sixteen hundred people by telephone to gauge various populations' attitudes toward Simpson and trial evidence. According to Dimitrius, one significant finding "was that black females were much more neutral on the issue of abuse and domestic violence than perhaps a white female would be." This information encouraged the defense to use their peremptory challenges in a way that retained black female jurors, thereby reducing the chances of Simpson's abusive behavior becoming a significant issue during jury deliberations.

Many jury-system critics, however, claim that peremptory challenges are too often the result of racial, class, and sex discrimination. Jo-Ellan Dimitrius herself admits that she often relies on "some sort of stereotype" in her recommendations to lawyers. The use of prejudice is standard practice during the jury-screening process, critics argue, and frequently results in a jury that is not impartial and that delivers an unjust verdict. Furthermore, as Stephen Adler, author of *The Jury*, points out, peremptory challenges deny the rights of some segments of the population to participate in the judicial process: "If a defense lawyer excludes all Irish Americans because 'they' tend to be proprosecution, Irish Americans lose the opportunity to serve as jurors."

Such criticism of the peremptory challenge reached the U.S. Supreme Court in the 1986 case of *Batson v. Kentucky*. In that case, the Supreme Court ruled that prosecutors could no longer use race-based peremptory challenges to keep members of the defendant's race off the jury. Another Supreme Court case in 1992, *Georgia v. McCollum*, similarly barred defense lawyers from using peremptory challenges to exclude members of the plaintiff's race from the jury. Additionally, in 1994, the Court's *J.E.B. (James E. Bowman v. Alabama)* decision declared that lawyers could not exercise gender-based peremptory challenges. Despite these rulings, however, lawyers are still allowed to use peremptory strikes for race- and gender-neutral reasons, and critics of peremptory challenges insist that discriminatory strikes still occur. In one 1995 case, when peremptory strikes of two prospective black jurors were challenged, the prosecutors maintained that they wanted to exclude the jurors not because they were black but because they had beards. After the Supreme Court upheld the prosecutors' claim in *Purkett v. Elem*, Vanderbilt University law professor Nancy King commented that "now . . . any race-neutral reason [for excluding jurors] will probably fly."

Lawyers are rarely required to provide reasons for peremptory challenges, however, and many jury-system critics argue that it is impossible to know whether challenges are based on prejudice or bias. Therefore, they contend, it would be better to simply eliminate peremptory challenges entirely. Ridding the jury-screening process of peremptory challenges would, in their opinion, ensure jury impartiality and increase public confidence in the jury system.

The proposal to eliminate peremptory challenges is just one of the many suggested jury-system reforms being debated. The authors in *At Issue: The Jury System* discuss the benefits and the shortcomings of trial by jury and explore the various reform proposals that continue to be the center of controversy in both the legal community and the public sector.

1

The Jury System: An Overview

Kenneth Jost

Kenneth Jost is a staff writer for CQ Researcher, *a weekly report on current social issues. He has also written several articles on the judicial system for* ABA Journal.

The U.S. jury system experienced profound changes in the last three decades of the twentieth century. These changes include more diversification in jury pools, jurors' heightened awareness of the effect of publicity on high-profile cases, and increased juror receptivity to defense arguments. Some legal experts, however, believe that the jury system needs further reform. Suggested reforms include eliminating peremptory challenges, allowing majority verdicts, and giving jurors a more active role in trials. Opponents of such reforms argue that modifying the jury system may be harmful to the judicial process. Many experts agree, though, that the effectiveness of the jury system has increasingly become the subject of public concern, which may affect future jury-reform legislation.

When a jury in Prince George's County, Md., met in October 1995 to consider a three-count drug and firearms case against Kareem Brooks, 11 of the members were convinced of the defendant's guilt. But Walter Charles Boyd was not.

"Remember the O.J. Simpson case," Boyd told his fellow jurors. The 41-year-old medical supply salesman had watched much of the Simpson murder trial. And, as he told reporters later, the trial taught him something about the criminal justice system.

"I wanted the jurors to consider the fact that the evidence was not presented in a way that it should have been presented as far as the police officers gathering the evidence to prove the guilt of Mr. Brooks," Boyd said in an Oct. 13, 1995, television interview.[1]

Police in Prince George's County, a predominantly black suburb of Washington, D.C., said they arrested Brooks after seeing him drop a handgun and a vial of cocaine. But Boyd, who grew up in South Central

Los Angeles, agreed with the public defender's argument that police should have examined the gun for Brooks' fingerprints to corroborate their testimony.

The other members of the racially mixed jury insisted the officers' testimony was strong enough. At one point, they prevailed on Boyd to vote to convict. But he changed his mind on the way to the courtroom and told the clerk who polled the jurors that the verdict did not reflect his views.

Circuit Judge William B. Spellbring ordered the panel to resume deliberations, but it was no use. Boyd stuck to his position, and two hours later the foreman reported the jury was hopelessly deadlocked.[2]

Some law enforcement–minded experts . . . believe that juries are more suspicious of police and prosecutors than in the past.

For many Americans, Boyd had drawn the right lessons from the Simpson case: the need for jurors to be skeptical of law enforcement and serious about their own responsibilities. But for many others, the Simpson case represented everything that is wrong with the jury system: protracted trials, manipulative lawyers and erratic verdicts based more on emotion and prejudice than on thoughtful deliberation about evidence and the law.

Whatever one's opinion of the verdict in the Simpson case, the nine-month trial focused attention on the U.S. jury system in a way that no previous case had ever done. Critics of the jury system say that attention may be a boon to efforts to make some changes. "One of the things that the Simpson trial did was bring the issue of jury reform beyond the legal profession," says Stephen J. Adler, special projects editor at the *Wall Street Journal* and author of a widely noted book on the jury system.[3] "More people are looking at jury reform as a sort of public interest issue, not an inside baseball issue."

Adler says the Simpson case underscores the need to simplify jury selection procedures by eliminating "peremptory challenges," which give lawyers the right to exclude juror candidates for almost any reason.

Other critics say the trial highlights the need to radically simplify procedures during the trial itself. "The jury system is so complex, so expensive, so time-consuming that we cannot afford to give it to more than a handful of people," says John Langbein, a professor at Yale Law School. Langbein favors replacing the adversary procedures used in the United States with a system of judicially supervised investigations and trials like those in many European countries.

Some experts caution against using the Simpson case to draw any lessons about the jury system. "The Simpson case is [such] an anomaly that we cannot generalize from it," says Lois Heaney, a jury consultant with the defense-oriented National Jury Project in Oakland, Calif.

Lawyers and experts alike agree that the jury system has undergone some dramatic changes within the last 30 years. Thanks to broadened selection procedures, juries are more diverse than in the past. Thanks to television coverage of trials, juries also appear to be more conscious of public attention in high-profile cases.[4] And, according to some experts, jurors in this law-and-order era are, paradoxically, somewhat more receptive to defense lawyers' arguments in the courtroom than in the past.

Alan M. Dershowitz, the Harvard Law School professor and criminal defense lawyer, wrote in 1994 that juries are too ready to accept what he called "abuse excuse" defenses—a tactic of claiming a history of abuse as an excuse for violent retaliation.[5] Dershowitz cited as examples the defenses presented by two California brothers, Eric and Lyle Menendez, for the 1989 slayings of their parents, and by Lorena Bobbitt for cutting off her husband's penis in 1993.

Many experts doubt Dershowitz's thesis that such defenses are either common or commonly successful. "Despite occasional success, the bottom line is that juries are just as hostile to mental health excuses or defenses as they have been in the past," says Valerie Hans, a professor of legal studies at the University of Delaware.

Some law enforcement–minded experts, however, do believe that juries are more suspicious of police and prosecutors than in the past. "There is a greater degree of distrust of authority," says Gerard Lynch, a professor at Columbia Law School and former federal prosecutor. "It shows up much more in the typical narcotics case, where no one is raising a defense that they were an abused child but they're saying that the police are lying."

While law enforcement personnel may chafe under the heightened scrutiny, some experts applaud the changes that more diverse juries have brought about. "The jury is more truly representative of the public than it ever has been before in history," says Hans. "To the extent that the jury represents a broader range of people, we might have more hung juries or greater difficulty in arriving at a collective and unanimous decision. [But] I would say that represents a success for the jury as a decision-making body."

The Simpson case also focused new attention on the issue of race in criminal trials. Jurors on the panel—all but three of them black—insisted afterward that race had not been a factor in their decision to find Simpson not guilty of the killings of his former wife, Nicole Brown Simpson, and her friend, Ronald Goldman.

> *The jury is more truly representative of the public than it ever has been before in history.*

Nonetheless, the verdicts came at a time when one black law professor was urging African-American jurors to make greater use of the controversial doctrine of "jury nullification"—which permits a jury to acquit a defendant even if there is sufficient evidence of guilt.

Debates over the jury system are nothing new, of course. Mark Twain satirized the American system of jury selection in an 1871 account of a murder trial. After reputable townsfolk were all excluded from the jury because they had read accounts of the case, Twain concluded: "Ignoramuses alone could mete out unsullied justice."[6]

Most of the debate about the jury system in the 1980s focused on the civil justice system. Business groups complained of escalating jury awards in an expanding array of personal injury lawsuits and, in the face of stren-

uous opposition from plaintiffs lawyers and consumer groups, won en-
actment of damage limits in many states. By the 1990s, the debate about
juries had shifted to the criminal justice system—most notably, because
of an all-white jury's acquittal of four Los Angeles police officers in the
beating of a black motorist, Rodney King, in 1991.

Through all the debate, judges and other court officials have been
concentrating on the less glamorous work of trying to make juries more
representative and jury service more attractive and less onerous for the
millions of Americans summoned for jury duty each year. New York is
one of many states currently working to reach more people by using
sources other than the traditional voter lists to summon jurors. And Arizona is instituting a new set of jury reform measures aimed at giving jurors a more active role during trials by encouraging note-taking, questions
and even deliberations before the end of the trial.

As these varied efforts at improving the jury system continue, what
follows are some of the issues being debated.

Peremptory challenges

The jury system came to America from England three centuries ago, but
today jury procedures in the two countries are strikingly different in
many ways. The greatest contrast, perhaps, is the length of time required
to pick a jury.

Jury selection in England is short and sweet. Lawyers cannot question
the potential jurors and cannot excuse anyone from service except for a
specific legal ground. In the United States, on the other hand, jury selection can last days or even weeks and is often contentious. Lawyers and
the judge often question jurors extensively about their knowledge of a
case, their backgrounds and their views on legal and social issues. And
both the court and the opposing attorneys excuse people from serving in
almost any major case.

Many potential jurors are disqualified for some legal reason. These so-
called "for cause" challenges may be based on a juror's knowledge of the
case or a professed inability to follow applicable law. But lawyers also
have the right to use so-called "peremptory challenges" to exclude a certain number of potential jurors for any reason—or for no reason at all.

Trial lawyers cherish the peremptory challenge. "Peremptories offer
an opportunity for the litigators to exercise challenges that are not traditionally recognized by the law for cause but can eliminate people who are
unwilling or unable to listen to one or both sides of the case," says G.
Marc Whitehead, a Minneapolis attorney who chairs the American Bar
Association's task force on juries.

A growing number of jury reformers, however, favor limiting or eliminating peremptory challenges. They say the arbitrary exclusion of potential jurors insults the people who are called to jury duty and lowers
public confidence in the overall fairness of the jury system.

"Obviously, [peremptories] are great things for lawyers," says Albert
Alschuler, a law professor at the University of Chicago. "They let the me-
ter run longer. They play great strategic games. Every lawyer believes he
or she is a master of the art of jury selection. But there is no empirical evidence to suggest that it makes any difference in the art of jury selection."

"Many of those who are currently removed via lawyers' challenges appear to be more alert and unbiased than many who are seated," Adler writes. "And many peremptory challenges continue to be rooted in racial, ethnic and sex discrimination."[7]

The Supreme Court has acted in the past decade to limit some discriminatory uses of peremptory challenges. In 1986, the court ruled in a case called *Batson v. Kentucky* that prosecutors cannot use peremptory challenges to exclude potential jurors on the basis of race. The justices later extended the ruling to bar race-based peremptory challenges in civil cases and by defense lawyers in criminal cases. Then in 1994, the court also prohibited lawyers from excluding jurors on account of their gender.

The decisions stoked speculation that the justices might abolish peremptories altogether. "This is the death knell for the peremptory strike," Bruce Harvey, a criminal defense attorney in Atlanta, told the *ABA Journal* in advance of the ruling barring gender-based challenges.[8]

On each occasion, however, the court insisted that lawyers could continue to use peremptory challenges for other reasons. And in 1995, the court gave lawyers added leeway in justifying peremptory challenges that are challenged as discriminatory.

In a little noticed, unsigned decision, *Purkett v. Elem*, the court said that a lawyer's reason for excusing a juror can pass muster if it is race-neutral even if it is not reasonable. The May 15, 1995, decision upheld a prosecutor's use of peremptory challenges to remove two black jurors, ostensibly because they had mustaches or beards. "Now the court has said that any race-neutral reason will probably fly," says Nancy King, an associate professor of law at Vanderbilt University who has written extensively on juries and peremptory challenges.

Lawyers on both sides of the table continue to defend peremptory challenges. Elizabeth Semel, a criminal defense lawyer in San Diego, says peremptory challenges are often needed to excuse jurors who cannot accept that a defendant is presumed innocent. "Sometimes the only way you can excuse them from a jury is through a peremptory challenge," she says.

A growing number of jury reformers . . . favor limiting or eliminating peremptory challenges.

Greg Totten, executive director of the California District Attorneys Association, says prosecutors also want to retain the peremptory challenge. "I think most prosecutors think there is value to peremptory challenges and would not want to see them eliminated," he says.

Critics acknowledge that lawyers' unified stance on peremptory challenges makes any change difficult, if not impossible. Typically, state law establishes the right to peremptory challenges and prescribes the number—ranging from as low as two or three per side in civil cases to as many as 25 in capital cases. Prosecutors, defense attorneys and civil trial lawyers on both sides would be likely to resist any legislation to reduce the number or abolish peremptories altogether.

Still, critics say public discontent with jury selection procedures has increased because of high-publicity trials like the Simpson case. "The distress that people have about the O.J. verdict and other verdicts has people concerned about lawyers stacking juries through the use of jury consultants," Alschuler says. "One way to reduce that concern is to eliminate peremptory challenges."

The ABA's Whitehead insists that opposition to peremptory challenges is "very much a political thing" and is likely to fade over time. But Adler says the political climate surrounding lawyers could allow restrictive legislation to pass. "Anti-lawyer sentiment is so intense that it should not theoretically be impossible to do something that lawyers oppose," he says.

Non-unanimous verdicts

The very first juries—the ancient Greek assemblages of 500 or more persons called dicasteries—decided disputes by majority vote. English courts, however, adopted a rule by the 14th century requiring jury verdicts to be unanimous. The unanimity requirement moved to America and became a central element of the U.S. jury system.

The Supreme Court in 1972, however, upheld laws in two states, Oregon and Louisiana, permitting criminal verdicts by 10-2 or 9-3 votes, respectively. Today, about half the states allow juries to decide civil cases by a less-than-unanimous vote. Now, prosecutors in California plan to ask voters in 1996 to permit 10-2 verdicts in all criminal trials except death penalty cases.

The proposal is part of the so-called Public Safety Protection Act of 1996, a ballot initiative currently being circulated for signatures. Greg Totten, executive director of the California District Attorneys Association, the chief sponsor of the measure, says the proposal would put more criminals in prison for longer sentences and save the legal system time and the expense of costly retrials.

"The unanimity requirement is like a cloud hanging over the criminal justice system," Totten says. In addition to forcing retrials in cases of jury deadlocks, he says the rule also affects plea bargaining by forcing prosecutors and courts to agree to less serious charges. "It puts dangerous criminals back on the street at an earlier point than we would if we could convict on the basis of 10 of 12 jurors," Totten says.

Defense lawyers and many jury experts strongly oppose the idea. They say that the proposal not only would give prosecutors a big advantage over the current system but also would result in less deliberation among jurors. "One of the chief advantages of a jury over an individual decisionmaker is the notion of deliberation," Adler says. "The problem with going to a 10-2 or 9-3 verdict is it encourages juries to vote, not to deliberate."

Semel, co-chair of the National Association of Criminal Defense Lawyers' legislative committee, agrees. "It's extremely important for every one of those 12 members to feel that each one must be attentive, each one must listen," she says. Eliminating the unanimity requirement, she says, "will marginalize the minority—whoever on the jury looks least like the other 11."

Hans at the University of Delaware says the focus on the impact of race in jury deliberations has made retaining the unanimity requirement more important. "Race does make a difference" in the jury room, Hans says. Retaining the unanimity requirement "means that you won't allow the verdict to reflect the racial breakdown. That would be a real disservice to the jury system."

For their part, prosecutors insist that permitting a verdict on a 10-2 vote would eliminate the danger that one or two "aberrant" jurors can prevent a panel from reaching a decision. Although statistics on hung juries are imprecise, California seemingly has a higher rate than other states. The state district attorneys' group says that Los Angeles County has had a hung jury rate of about 14 percent between 1992 and 1995, compared with 5 percent in Oregon, with its 10-2 verdict requirement.[9]

Totten says the change would affect perhaps as many as half of the juries that now end in deadlock and could also make some defense attorneys more likely to settle other cases. "The defense lawyer is not going to be rewarded for taking a guilty defendant to trial in hopes of getting one aberrant juror to hang it up," Totten says.

The prosecutors group also cites potential cost savings from avoiding the need for retrials in cases that end in deadlock. "It costs the taxpayers approximately $10,000 per day to have a jury trial conducted," Totten says. "And many of these cases that result in hung juries need to be retried, at tremendous cost."

A coalition of law enforcement and crime victims' groups began planning for the initiative after the state Assembly's public safety committee rejected 10-2 verdicts on a 4-4 vote in April 1995. The state's Republican governor, Pete Wilson, endorsed the measure in August. Interest in the idea grew in September as observers began speculating on the possibility of a hung jury in the Simpson trial. But the jurors' quick agreement on a verdict ended any possibility of using the case as a talking point in the campaign.

Totten stresses, however, that California prosecutors were urging non-unanimous verdicts long before the Simpson case. He says that both Louisiana and Oregon appear to be satisfied with their systems. And he notes that England moved to allow non-unanimous verdicts in 1967.

The role of jurors

Jurors today have a largely passive role in trials. They listen silently to testimony, pass in and out of the courtroom when told, and, if they follow instructions, avoid any discussion of the case until the trial has ended. When the ancestor of the U.S. jury system was being born in England nine centuries ago, however, jurors played a more active part.

English juries then consisted of neighbors summoned by the sheriff to decide a dispute on the basis of their own knowledge and investigation. Over time, the role of witnesses, lawyers and judges became more important, and the jurors' responsibilities lessened. Nonetheless, as late as the 1600s, English jurors retained discretion to ask questions during trial without permission.

Arizona Superior Court Judge B. Michael Dann, a leading advocate of jury reform, cites that history in arguing for giving today's jurors a more active role during the trial. "Jurors must be allowed greater roles in trials," Dann wrote in an influential law review article in 1993, "if juries are to remain up to the task of resolving today's disputes and if the institution of trial by jury is to retain its vitality."[10]

Dann headed a committee appointed by the Arizona Supreme Court that fashioned a set of jury reforms that took effect on Dec. 1, 1995. The proposals are aimed at helping jurors understand a trial while in progress by encouraging note-taking, permitting jurors to ask questions and having lawyers and the judge give interim summations and instructions. Most controversially, the proposal permits jurors in civil cases to discuss evidence among themselves during the trial.

Public discontent with jury selection procedures has increased because of high-publicity trials like the [O.J.] Simpson case.

Many of the proposals find broad support among judges and lawyers, even though they differ with trial practices used in most places until recently. Juror note-taking, for example, has traditionally been viewed with suspicion. Judges and lawyers feared that a juror's notes might taint or unduly influence the deliberations. But note-taking has become common today, and none of the lawyers, judges or experts interviewed for this report objected to the practice.

Allowing jurors to ask questions raises greater concerns. The Arizona plan calls for jurors to submit unsigned written questions to the judge, who would ask the questions after giving lawyers an opportunity to object outside the presence of the jury. Supporters believe that jurors will have a better opportunity to understand complex testimony if they can ask their own questions.

Still, some lawyers doubt that jurors will ask many useful questions and warn that they may ask improper ones. "It's important to remember who's trying the lawsuit: the lawyers and the judge," says defense attorney Semel. "Sometimes a juror asks a question about an item of evidence that has been properly excluded. But there may be a time when a question has been well founded and is appropriate."

Dann concedes that the practice requires careful judicial supervision. "The judge is going to have to ride herd on that process," he says. "It can get out of hand. But that's no different from controlling other aspects of the trial."

The plan to invite jurors to discuss evidence with the trial still in progress provokes more divided opinions. Dann and others say that jurors will benefit from talking about a case with the evidence fresh in their minds. "Real-time discussions will aid the comprehension, aid in formulating the questions that they ask and assist in reducing stress because they are able to talk to each other aside from small talk," Dann says.

In any event, Dann and other supporters of the idea say that many jurors ignore the admonition not to talk about a case during the trial. In its report on jury reform, Dann's committee noted research suggesting that anywhere from 11 percent to 40 percent of jurors discuss evidence among themselves before deliberations.[11]

Some law professors agree that it is unrealistic to expect jurors to avoid talking about a case until the end of a trial. "It's a bad dynamic to tell them something that may not be realistic," says Columbia's Lynch.

Trial lawyers, however, voiced nearly uniform opposition to the plan. Whitehead, head of the ABA's task force on juries, says he bases his opposition on studies by social scientists that indicate people tend to hold to an opinion after once publicly expressing it.

"They get concerned that interim discussions solidify thinking prior to hearing all the evidence, that interim discussions foreclose debate because the discussions do not necessarily happen with the whole group present and that interim discussions will result in sides being taken and groups formed," Whitehead says.

Defense lawyer Semel maintains that interim discussions would be particularly dangerous in criminal cases. "The presumption of innocence is supposed to apply literally through the entire trial," Semel says. "The idea of interim deliberations is a way of undermining that presumption prematurely."

The plan to invite jurors to discuss evidence with the trial still in progress provokes . . . divided opinions.

For the time being, Arizona will limit interim discussions to civil cases. Dann favors extending the idea to criminal cases, but acknowledges a reason for caution. "There are some legitimate concerns and weightier concerns on criminal [cases] than on civil [ones]," he says. "We should wait and see how it works."

Nonetheless, Dann says that jurors in cases where the idea has been tested have told him they did not form hard opinions before the trial ended. "They rather convincingly reassure and even scold me for even thinking that they would rush to judgment before they hear all the evidence," Dann says.

Notes

1. Brooks appeared on ABC's "Good Morning America," Oct. 13, 1995. For details of the case, see the *Prince Georges Journal*, Oct. 12, 1995, p. A1; and *The Washington Post*, Oct. 12, 1995, p. B1.

2. An earlier trial also ended with a deadlocked jury. A new court hearing was scheduled for Dec. 1, 1995.

3. See Stephen J. Adler, *The Jury: Trial and Error in the American Courtroom* (1994).

4. For background, see "Courts and the Media," *CQ Researcher*, Sept. 23, 1994, pp. 817–840.

5. Alan M. Dershowitz, *The Abuse Excuse: And Other Cop-Outs, Sob Stories and Evasions of Responsibility* (1994). Dershowitz's original column on the abuse excuse, written in January 1994, appears at pp. 45–47.

6. Mark Twain, *Roughing It* (1903 ed., vol. 2), p. 75, cited in Jeffrey Abramson, *We, the Jury: The Jury System and the Ideal of Democracy* (1994), p. 45.

7. Stephen J. Adler, "Blueprints for Building a Better Jury System," *The Wall Street Journal*, Sept. 14, 1994, B12. See also Adler, *op. cit.*, pp. 221–224.

8. Quoted in Mark Curriden, "The Death of the Peremptory Challenge," *ABA Journal*, January 1994, p. 62.

9. California District Attorneys Association, "Non-Unanimous Jury Verdicts: A Necessary Criminal Justice Reform," May 8, 1995, Appendix C.

10. B. Michael Dann, "'Learning Lessons' and 'Speaking Rights': Creating Educated and Democratic Juries," *Indiana Law Journal*, vol. 68, no. 4, fall 1993, p. 1230.

11. Arizona Supreme Court Committee on More Effective Use of Juries, "The Power of 12," November 1994, p. 97 n. 65. Two sources were cited: Loftus & Leber, "Do Jurors Talk," *Trial*, January 1986, p. 60; Note, "Jurors Judge Justice: A Survey of Criminal Jurors," *New Mexico Law Review*, 1973, p. 358.

2

Trial by Jury Should Be Abolished

Christie Davies

Christie Davies is a sociology professor at the University of Reading in England and the coauthor of Wrongful Imprisonment: Mistaken Convictions and Their Consequences.

Most states do not set standards for juror suitability. Instead, prosecutors and defense lawyers are allowed to question individual jurors, enabling them to try to pick jurors who will agree with their side. This process undermines the ideal of random selection of a jury. However, even randomly chosen jurors would not guarantee a careful verdict: Certain jurors may be capable and intelligent, while others may be careless and uninformed. Because of juror unreliability, juries often acquit criminals and convict innocent people. Justice would be better served if a small team of judges and other legal professionals rendered verdicts, while juries of peers only decided on sentencing.

In all the wringing of hands about race, civil rights, and the relations between police and public occasioned by the Rodney King verdicts, no one has dared to criticize that sacred cow, "trial by jury." No institution competing in the marketplace would ever survive if at its core it had a system of decision-making like this, one which is about as reliable as an examination of the entrails of a ritually sacrificed free-range rooster.

Behind each erroneous conviction there lies a muddled jury of 12 more or less good, supposedly true, men, women, and hobbledehoys. Since most states do not demand any kind of qualification based on property or education, the dullest citizens may sit on a jury. Juries are also erratically skewed by the attempts by prosecution, and even more by defense, lawyers to cross-examine, challenge, and choose individual jurors until they get the jury composition they want, a process made even easier if they can also choose *where* the trial is held. In so doing they undermine the very rationale of the jury as a random representation of the people at large. The very principle of the random selection of jurors is itself a

Christie Davies, "Trial by Judges," *National Review*, May 24, 1993; ©1993 by National Review, Inc., 150 E. 35th St., New York, NY 10016. Reprinted by permission.

dubious one for other reasons. No one in his senses would entrust an important decision in his life—where to live, what job to apply for, whether to have an operation, what shares to buy—to a random sample of 12 people, and yet we place our system of criminal justice in their uncertain hands. In some districts, no doubt, the jurors are above average, but in others they are stupid, feckless, illiterate, and felonious in thought and undetected deed. Does it really redress the balance if these same wretched jurors are mugged and raped on their way home by the villains they have just acquitted?

Jurors make wrong decisions

Not only do jurors wrongly acquit, they also falsely convict, and there are many innocent men and women sitting in jails throughout America because a jury got it wrong. The studies of wrongful imprisonment by Edward Radin, Edwin M. Borchard, Jerome and Barbara Frank, E.S. Gardner, and E.B. Block cite a frightening number of such cases. In addition to the famous instances they discuss, there are many other unknown, not very articulate, wrongly imprisoned individuals whose plight is not going to gain the attention of legal crusaders or those with influence in the mass media. They are alleged rapists who have been set up by vindictive women whose favors they once enjoyed but later spurned. They are small-businessmen done for "serious" fraud who were quite incapable of keeping one set of account books let alone two. They are all unfashionable little people, and no newspaper or television station is going to invest substantial sums of money in investigating their cases. They are all in prison because juries are no shrewder or more experienced than you or I and usually a lot less so.

Should these unfortunates take their case to appeal, they will get nowhere, because appeals courts see their task as being to look for minor and irrelevant errors in legal procedure rather than to re-examine the facts, however flagrantly absurd the jury's verdict may have been. Appeals courts may be barred by the state constitution from considering questions of fact at all, and, even when they are allowed to do so, they are reluctant to declare that the jury got it wrong. Even if in private the appeals judges think that the jurors were dolts, they will not say so, but will scrabble around trying to find a minor procedural error that will allow them to set aside the verdict. The worst position for an innocent defendant to be in is for the trial to be conducted impeccably and for the jury then perversely to convict. The appeals judges are then unable to criticize the trial procedure and will not criticize the jury, so the defendant stays in prison.

There are many innocent men and women sitting in jails throughout America because a jury got it wrong.

The jury is quite unlike all other tribunals, which have to give reasons for their decisions and to show how evidence is linked by logic to produce a conclusion. The jury is an oracle, a secret anonymous conclave swayed by unknown and unknowable prejudices and mental aberrations. Its decisions cannot be criticized or easily overturned because no one has any idea how it arrived at them. For appeals judges to speculate too much on the perceptions and reasoning of jurors would be to rob the jury of its primitive sacred quality. So they have no choice but to hide behind these bookless sibyls or to attack, sometimes unfairly, their judicial colleague's handling of the original trial.

If we are to have a rational method of reaching verdicts in criminal trials that also gives proper scope for appeal, then the jury must be replaced by a small team of experienced professional legal assessors. They would have to provide open, reasoned, and explicit reports saying how and why they reached their verdict.

Judge and jury should swap roles

The jury, however, ought to be retained in some capacity, as it is a part of democracy, a means of involving the ordinary citizen in the making of decisions within the criminal-justice system. The task for which the jury *is* eminently suited is that of sentencing. Juries should be entrusted with the task of deciding what penalty (within limits laid down by the state legislatures) should be imposed on those convicted by the new tribunals described above. Judge and jury should thus swap places.

Judges are by virtue of their training and experience better at deciding questions of fact as well as law than are the inexperienced members of a jury. However, when it comes to sentencing, judges are sometimes quirky and erratic and hand out bizarre sentences that indicate their ignorance of the moral priorities of the mass of the population. This situation can be rectified by letting the jury decide the sentence. The jury, being a random sample of the public, by definition represents the moral indignation of the community at large far better than any panel of judges, criminologists, or market researchers could ever do. Individual men and women differ enormously in intellectual capacity and thus in their ability to arrive at a correct decision, but they are democratically though arbitrarily equal in their power of telling right from wrong. In a democracy consciences are equal, however unequal brains may be. Not cloistered judges out of touch with popular sentiment but the people themselves should assess the heinousness of particular crimes and thus the appropriate sentence. Let the judges become the jury and the jury the judges.

3

The Jury System Should Be Retained

Barbara Allen Babcock

Barbara Allen Babcock is a law professor at Stanford University and a former assistant attorney general under the Carter administration.

Although juries sometimes make mistakes or decide on verdicts with which the public disagrees, there is no need to abolish or overhaul the jury system. Suggested reforms to the jury—such as allowing majority verdicts, reducing the number of jurors, and abolishing peremptory challenges—may harm rather than improve the system. More often than not, a jury's decision serves justice. The jury is a crucial part of a legal system that protects the democratic freedoms of all Americans.

"I personally would have a reasonable doubt, but it's true there is overwhelming evidence that he is possibly guilty."

This statement by an African-American man, interviewed on TV shortly before the verdict in the O.J. Simpson double-murder trial, reveals the tension inherent in our jury system. "Overwhelming evidence" may lead only to the "possibility" of guilt, and in its face, the jury may still entertain sufficient reservations to acquit.

Juries may also make mistakes, may be swayed by passion, prejudice and sympathy to acquit a guilty person; may misread the evidence, or misconstrue their duty. The first Simpson jurors to speak out seem to be saying that they took quite literally the judge's instruction that they might discount totally the evidence of police officers who lied in some respects. In a sense, they may have become the enforcers of exclusionary rules that many judges no longer follow. Even as individual jurors come forward, however, we are not likely to fully understand the dynamics that led to Simpson's acquittal.

But all who think, as I do, that this verdict is wrong, should not turn their frustration and anger on the criminal jury system itself. Far worse than letting a guilty man go free would be losing faith in, or working fundamental changes on, this most American of institutions.

Barbara Allen Babcock, "Protect the Jury System, Judge Was the Problem," *Los Angeles Times*, October 8, 1995. Reprinted by permission of the author.

22

Even before the Simpson verdicts were in, partly in response to the first Rodney G. King–beating case and the Menendez hung jury, there were legislative moves afoot in California: to do away with the unanimity requirement; to reduce the number of jurors; to abolish peremptory challenges. There are two basic problems with these proposals: First, they rest on a faulty premise that the jury system is broken, and, second, they have the potential to change its operation profoundly in unpredictable ways.

The price of liberty

That the jury may make mistakes—or may express through its verdict community sentiment that is, at best, extra-legal—is part of the system, part of the price we pay to have a judgment of the people before we deprive anyone of all liberty. We have always, from the founding of the republic, been willing to sustain the risk that a jury will be wrong. Nothing in the Simpson verdicts changes that.

For every jury that goes awry, there are a hundred that do the right thing. Lawyers on both sides of the criminal system, former jurors and most academics who have studied juries, attest to this. I believe in juries based on my experience as a young lawyer, when I tried many cases—losing some and winning others, representing mostly African-American men before mostly African-American juries in Washington.

Though losing a verdict is one of life's crushing blows, in virtually all cases I saw close up, the jury made a correct, and wise, decision. More than occasionally, I found that jurors who started with one predisposition—sometimes ones I had chosen because I discerned it—changed their minds through the deliberations.

But no jury in my experience was so mistreated and abused as the Simpson jury. Indeed, it might well be that the mismanagement of the jury helped produce the acquittal. This is the second reason why this case should not be an occasion for sweeping changes: the law of unintended consequences.

For every jury that goes awry, there are a hundred that do the right thing.

We do not know what makes juries work well most of the time—which feature is necessary to proper functioning. The jury comes with certain historical attributes: the mystical number 12; the absolute power, without accountability, to acquit; the judicial filtering of the evidence they will hear; the absence of merit-type qualifications of education or training for service; the requirement that they engage each other to the point of total agreement. No one knows which, if any, of these is essential to the integrity of the institution.

We do know, however, that a jury should be a group put together once in time for a single purpose, that it should be composed of strangers, who know each other only through their deliberations.

This fundamental feature was violated in the Simpson case by a starstruck judge who lost control of the situation. Judge Lance A. Ito caused the jury to spend many hours waiting while he heard and reheard lawyers' arguments, took time off to engage celebrities and, through it all, patronized the jurors—conveying by his tone and manner that their time was not important. He should have taken drastic measures to move the trial along—for example, he might have heard motions in the evenings, and held court on Saturdays. Instead, by his leisurely approach, he violated the very premises of the jury and permitted the possibility that they would become a little band with their own agenda.

Legal statutes and their consequences

But Ito, like the judges in most states, was largely on his own in deciding how to deal with this jury. The statutes, and common law, on the selection, care and instruction of juries are a hodgepodge of piecemeal rules—some adopted in reaction to unpopular verdicts—without concern for how the system, as a whole, will be affected. The most recent addition, for instance, imposed by initiative, removed the right of lawyers to question potential jurors. By the report of both prosecutors and defenders, the unintended consequence of this law has been a dramatic increase in hung juries—because lawyers on both sides are unable to uncover through follow-up questions and direct contact, those who may prove to be unreasoning outliers in jury deliberation.

Rather than such reactive legislation, a comprehensive statute that preserved the jury's basic attributes would be a good outcome of the Simpson verdicts. Such a statute should include, for example, provisions regularizing selection practices, including juror questionnaires tailored to the facts of the individual cases; provision for expedited procedures in cases of sequestration, and for more reasonable compensation and treatment of jurors.

Meanwhile, whether or not we agree with the Simpson verdict, all should accept and respect it. The criminal jury system, right or wrong, is still one of our greatest and most characteristically American institutions. Like universal suffrage—a vote for every citizen regardless of class, race or gender—the jury drawn from the community with absolute power to protect the accused from the state is fundamental to our democracy.

4

The Majority Verdict Should Be Adopted

Jacob Tanzer

Jacob Tanzer is a legal counselor to the law firm of Ball-Janik Limited Liability Partnership in Portland, Oregon. He is a former prosecutor, civil-rights lawyer, and Oregon State Supreme Court justice. Tanzer successfully argued for non-unanimous verdicts before the U.S. Supreme Court in the 1972 case of Apodaca v. Oregon.

Most states require jurors to reach a unanimous verdict in criminal cases. However, the unanimous-verdict system is flawed and often results in hung juries and retrials. Since 1934, Oregon has used a majority-verdict system that has proven effective in producing accurate convictions and acquittals. Under a majority-verdict system, jurors do not feel pressured to give up their personal opinions to reach an agreement. When jurors vote according to their true beliefs, the jury's verdict has more validity. The majority verdict should be adopted because it results in fewer hung juries and encourages jurors to retain their convictions as they make a final decision.

America has allowed less than unanimous verdicts for more than 200 years. James Madison wrote the Sixth Amendment to include a requirement for unanimous verdicts, but Congress deleted that provision before sending the Bill of Rights to the states for ratification. The reason: Four of 13 states did not require unanimity and Congress was disinclined to force them to do otherwise.

Oregon's super-majority jury system has worked well for half a century. At least 10 jurors must agree to a felony verdict. There are fewer hung juries and fewer retrials, and nobody has seriously claimed that guilty defendants are culled from the innocent less accurately in Oregon than elsewhere. Similarly, England and most of Australia allow super-majority verdicts and Scotland has traditionally required only 8 out of 15 jurors to reach a verdict. Nobody has suggested that juries in Oregon, England, Australia or Scotland produce less accurate decisions than elsewhere.

Jacob Tanzer, "Unanimity Isn't Human Nature," *Los Angeles Times*, August 18, 1995. Reprinted by permission of the author.

The historic reason for juries was to allow the people, rather than kings or even judges, to decide guilt or innocence. Juries began as gatherings of witnesses. For the people rather than the king to decide, however, it was not necessary for a particular number of jurors to agree. A super-majority of one's peers is a sturdy bulwark against oppression by the state.

Non-unanimous verdicts should not be considered a "get tough on crime" strategy. Jurors are not necessarily the prosecutor's friends. The question is whether super-majority verdicts improve the justice system. The answer is that they allow more accurate and more efficient decision-making by jurors, whether for convictions or acquittals. A study by the University of Chicago Law School showed that the ratio of convictions and acquittals was about the same under either system, but that the number of hung juries was reduced by more than 40% where 10 or 11 jurors could decide.

The problem with unanimous verdicts

The strategy of many defense lawyers, particularly when the prosecution's case is strong, is often not to seek an acquittal, but to hang the jury by choosing at least one juror with the temperament to hold out against the others and to convince this juror to do so. Such lawyers try their cases to one juror instead of to 12. I do not criticize defense lawyers for using every legal advantage for their clients, but there is something fundamentally wrong with a system of justice that makes indecision a victory. The purpose of a trial is to produce a decision. A hung jury is not a success for the jury system. To the contrary, a hung jury represents a failure of the justice system to produce a decision.

Perfect unanimity is simply not consistent with human nature. Seldom do 12 people hold the same opinion, particularly on grave matters. In ancient times, juries were starved into unanimity; often they were denied food and sleep until they reached a verdict. Today, jurors are sequestered together until they reach a unanimous verdict. Too often, they reach compromise verdicts instead of verdicts that truly reflect the convictions of the individual jurors. That is why armed robbers and rapists are sometimes convicted merely of assault. When the majority must compromise with an unreasonable, biased or screwball juror in order to reach a verdict, justice suffers. When jurors can vote their minds without the need to compromise, the verdict better reflects the truth.

> *[Non-unanimous verdicts] allow more accurate and more efficient decision-making by jurors.*

It is also argued that the super-majority system allows jurors to ignore the views of dissenters. That is contrary to my observations. Jurors are very conscientious about how they perform their responsibility. As a matter of human nature, they allow everybody to have his or her say, usually before they even take a vote. They strive hard for unanimous decisions even after 10 or 11 jurors have agreed. Majorities tend to return non-unanimous verdicts only when they believe that further discussion is futile.

In no other decision-making body, even those that make society's most important decisions, do we require 12 people to agree. In every collegial decision-making body, there is some allowance for difference of opinion, whether reasoned, biased or crackpot. Even the Supreme Court, deciding matters of life and death, is seldom unanimous. The important thing for criminal juries is that those who agree do so with a depth of personal belief that is beyond a reasonable doubt. To require that 10 or 11 people hearing conflicting evidence each bear the same opinion is a very high obstacle to injustice.

5

The Unanimous Verdict Should Be Retained

Jeffrey Abramson

Jeffrey Abramson is a professor of politics at Brandeis University in Massachusetts. He has served as a law clerk to the California State Supreme Court and as an assistant district attorney in Massachusetts. Abramson is also the author of several books, including We, the Jury: The Jury System and the Ideal of Democracy, *from which the following viewpoint is excerpted.*

Many people argue that the jury system would be improved if the unanimous-verdict requirement were replaced by a majority-verdict requirement. However, studies reveal that when jurors must reach a unanimous verdict, they spend more time in deliberation and engage in higher-quality discussions of the case. Furthermore, in a significant number of cases, a minority of jury members turns around an initial majority vote through the process of deliberation. Unanimous verdicts require jurors to actively reason with, learn from, and persuade one another as they work toward a final decision. Because this characteristic of the unanimous-verdict system ensures that most jury decisions are carefully considered, both jurors and the general public feel more confident about the validity of unanimous verdicts.

Practically speaking, what difference would it make if juries were permitted to render 9–3 or 10–2 verdicts rather than unanimous verdicts? In *Apodaca v. Oregon* and *Johnson v. Louisiana*, the Court surmised that the effects would be minimal. [In these two 1972 cases, the Supreme Court ruled that states are not required to follow the unanimous verdict tradition.] Presumably, there would be some reduction in hung juries and thus some gain in the efficiency of the system. But the Court thought neither the prosecution nor the defense would gain an edge from the shift.[1] Deliberation would proceed as before, and would be just as thorough, reliable, and representative of opposing points of view.

Even before the Court announced its decisions, social scientists were busy studying the effects of unanimity on jury behavior. In 1955, the University of Chicago Jury Project undertook the most massive field study of actual jury trials ever attempted in the United States. The project's original research plan called for secretly recording the actual deliberations of juries. With the consent of the trial judge and counsel but without the knowledge of the jurors, audio recordings were made in five civil cases in federal district court in Wichita, Kansas. But when word of such recordings became public in the summer of 1955, the U.S. attorney general publicly censured electronic "eavesdropping" on jury deliberations. Congress and more than thirty states responded by enacting statutes prohibiting jury tapings.[2] Ever since, jury deliberations have been secret. A rare exception occurred in 1986 when the Public Broadcasting System televised an authorized videotape of the actual deliberations of a Wisconsin criminal jury.[3]

Jurors returning nonunanimous verdicts [feel] far less certain of their conclusions than [do] their counterparts on unanimous verdict juries.

The Chicago Jury Project attempted to make a virtue out of its inability to study "the real thing." In 1966, principal authors Harry Kalven, Jr., and Hans Zeisel published much of the project's findings in *The American Jury*, the most influential book ever written on the subject. Kalven and Zeisel dismissed deliberation as having no significant effect on the final verdict in nine of every ten cases. "With very few exceptions," they wrote, "the first ballot determines the outcome of the verdict. . . . [T]he real decision is often made before the deliberation begins."[4]

More precisely, *The American Jury* presented data showing that "where there is an initial majority either for conviction or for acquittal, the jury in roughly nine out of ten cases decides in the direction of the initial majority."[5] This suggests that in 90 percent of the cases, the shift from a unanimous verdict requirement to a majority verdict rule would not change the eventual outcome. Kalven and Zeisel were brutally frank in debunking the romance surrounding deliberation and the arrival at unanimity. In their view, deliberation changed votes less through the force of reason and more through the peer pressure and intimidation that the initial majority mustered against holdouts. In other words, the achievement of unanimity should not delude us into regarding the verdict as more reliable; intimidation, not rational discussion, was the tactic through which the initial majority almost always prevailed in a small group situation.

The American Jury's debunking of deliberation and unanimity set the stage intellectually for the Supreme Court's refusal in 1972 to grant constitutional protection to the unanimous verdict. Why should law insist that unanimous verdicts are essential to justice, when science shows that the initial majority almost always prevails anyway? If the ideals of unanimity and deliberation, so lofty in theory, are reduced in practice to the dirty dynamics of majority pressure on a few holdouts in a small room, then why protect the rule that fuels the pressure?

And yet the implications of *The American Jury* for unanimous verdicts were not entirely negative. Even by their own statistics, Kalven and Zeisel recognized that "the minority eventually succeed[ed] in reversing an initial majority" in roughly 10 percent of sampled cases. Though at times they trivialized this figure (calling the percentage "very few exceptions"), they conceded that they "must not push the point [about the unimportance of unanimity and deliberation] too far." Cases where a minority turned a majority around "may be cases of special importance." They were also likely to be cases where the minority did have the stronger arguments and so were able to resist the normal tide of peer pressure. In these cases, the requirement of unanimity arguably permitted deliberation to continue long enough for reasoned argument to prevail over initial opinions.

Kalven and Zeisel also appreciated that less than unanimous verdicts would change the frequency of hung juries. Their sample included a small number of hung juries, whose last vote was known. By looking at the percentage of hung juries that were deadlocked by one or two jurors, the authors concluded that hung juries could be reduced 42 percent by permitting 11–1 or 10–2 verdicts. They arrived at a similar estimate by studying the frequency of hung juries among cases reported to them from jurisdictions that permitted less than unanimous verdicts at the time. In these majority verdict jurisdictions, hung juries occurred 3.1 percent of the time—a reduction of 45 percent from the national average of 5.6 percent in unanimous verdict jurisdictions.[6]

Since *The American Jury* was published, these estimates have been roughly confirmed by a study of hung juries in Multnomah County (Portland), Oregon, under that state's 10–2 rule. From 1970 to 1972, juries hung in only 2.5 percent of 801 criminal trials—a reduction slightly over 50 percent from the national average.[7]

Does such a reduction in hung juries favor either the prosecution or the defense? This is a difficult question to answer empirically because it is hard to have accurate information about what eventually happens to a defendant whose jury hangs. The state may pursue a new trial—winning, losing, or hanging again. Or the state may forgo retrial altogether. With this warning in mind, Kalven and Zeisel's statistics indicated that the state gained at least an immediate advantage from the decline in hung juries. The reason was that, among juries deadlocked at 11–1 or 10–2, the holdouts were more than four times more likely to be holding out for acquittal than for conviction. Under a 10–2 rule, therefore, far more split juries return convictions than acquittals.[8]

The Supreme Court's decisions in *Apodaca* and *Johnson* spurred social scientists into a new round of empirical studies of unanimous versus majority verdicts. In general, these studies have shown that "jury verdicts do not differ as a function of decision-rule"; the ratio of convictions to acquittals remains the same, whether mock juries are instructed to return unanimous verdicts or verdicts down to a two-thirds majority.[9] The only major difference, as far as final verdicts go, is that unanimous juries are more likely to hang.[10] All of this basically confirms Kalven and Zeisel's findings.

But, although the product of deliberation does not significantly change under nonunanimous verdict conditions, the process of deliberation apparently does. One of the key factual assumptions the Court made in abandoning the unanimous verdict requirement was that the thoroughness of deliberation would remain unchanged. Specifically, the Court counted on the fact that a majority faction would continue earnest deliberation with holdouts and not simply cut off debate once the required number of votes for a verdict had been attained. Various mock jury studies dispute this conclusion, showing a marked tendency of juries to "stop . . . the deliberation when the required number was reached."[11]

Public confidence in the accuracy of verdicts is greater when the verdict is unanimous.

In one simulation with names taken from actual jury lists, psychologist Reid Hastie and his colleagues studied the content of deliberation after eight jurors favored a verdict. On juries permitted to return an 8–4 verdict, "little occurs after the faction size reaches eight. . . . Deliberation continues for a few minutes, typically less than five." By contrast, on those juries required to reach unanimity, "approximately 20 percent of deliberation occurs after the largest faction contains eight or more members." Moreover, even if deliberation did continue on a jury that had reached the required eight-person majority, it never led to any desertions from the majority. And on seven of the twenty-three unanimous verdict juries studied, the largest faction reached eight but failed to render the final verdict.[12]

Such comparisons support the dissent of Justice William Douglas in *Apodaca*, when he argued for the difference between "polite" debate (which a majority might deign to have with minority jurors whose votes are not needed) and "robust" argument (which takes place when the majority needs to persuade the minority jurors). As sociologist Michael Saks put it, the achievement of the minimum bloc of votes necessary for a verdict is "psychologically binding" on bloc members. The deliberation may continue but it continues as an option, not an obligation.[13]

Various subsidiary findings support the general conclusion that deliberation between majority and minority factions becomes weak and watery once the majority has enough votes for a verdict. Kalven and Zeisel found that, under unanimous verdict rules, juries were hung by one or two jurors in only 2.4 percent of all cases.[14] Yet, in Oregon, which allows juries to return 10–2 verdicts, the number of juries rendering verdicts with one or two holdouts is 25 percent of all juries. This provides evidence that Oregon juries conclude their work rapidly once they achieve the required ten votes rather than pursuing deliberation in hopes of convincing the holdouts.[15] It seems reasonable to assume that jurors, missing paychecks and family, will adjourn as soon as the law authorizes them to return a verdict, rather than continuing extra deliberation.

Mock studies back up this assumption by showing a decline in deliberation time involving less than unanimous verdict conditions. The Hastie study in Massachusetts showed unanimous juries deliberating on average 138 minutes, juries deliberating only 103 minutes under a ten out of twelve rule, and juries deliberating 75 minutes under an eight out of twelve rule.[16] It is not surprising that the shorter deliberation time on majority verdict juries translated into less time spent correcting errors of fact and fewer requests for clarification of the judge's instructions.[17]

Finally, and most important, the empirical studies showed that jurors returning nonunanimous verdicts felt far less certain of their conclusions than did their counterparts on unanimous verdict juries.[18] This is so intuitively plausible that we probably did not need fancy mock jury studies to prove it: jurors not voting in favor of the majority's verdict are hardly likely to think justice was done. What is perhaps not so obvious is that the holdouts left the trial feeling that the majority did not even listen to them seriously. According to the Massachusetts study, the style of deliberation under nonunanimous verdict instructions was likely to be more combative than under unanimous rules, with "larger factions in majority rule juries adopt[ing] a more forceful, bullying, persuasive style because their members realize that it is not necessary to respond to all opposition arguments when their goal is to achieve a faction size of only eight or ten members."[19] One consequence was that members of nonunanimous verdict juries corrected each other's errors of fact less frequently, with those in the minority apparently concluding that the effort was unproductive.[20]

These research findings suggest that the quality of jury deliberation is far more tied to the practice of unanimous verdicts than the Supreme Court allowed in 1972. Moreover, because "popular acceptance of the jury system is formulated, in part, by what former jurors say about it, jurors' satisfaction is not without its importance."[21] All studies to date verify that juror satisfaction sours under nonunanimous verdict conditions. To this extent, the unanimous verdict rule must be seen as a core ingredient underwriting the jury's ability to legitimate justice in the eyes of the community.

Legitimacy, justice, and unanimity

As a matter of partisan politics, the campaign to abolish unanimous verdicts predictably divides public opinion along conservative versus liberal lines. For conservatives, the unanimous verdict requirement is a "law and order" issue—one feature among many that makes the jury system inefficient, wasteful, and prodefendant to a fault. In England, the telling argument against the unanimous verdict was that it had permitted some notorious defendants to walk free after successfully bribing a juror or two.[22]

In the United States, instances of jury tampering have been rare. And removal of the unanimous verdict is hardly likely to accomplish the other political reforms sought. Even under unanimous conditions, juries convict more than two of every three felony defendants—hardly a sign that juries coddle criminals.[23] All studies confirm that the ratio of convictions to acquittals would not significantly change under 9–3 or 10–2 verdict rules.[24]

As to efficiency, there would be a reduction in the frequency of hung juries, but even here the gains would be minimal. As we saw earlier, under a 10–2 verdict rule Multnomah County, Oregon, juries hang less than half as frequently as the national average—2.5 percent of all jury trials versus 5.6 percent nationally.[25] But in calculating the economic savings from this reduction, jury scholar Jon Van Dyke reminds us that jury trials are such a small percentage of total criminal dispositions in the first place that a small reduction in the already small number of hung juries would not have much influence on the overall efficiency of the system in resolving cases.[26]

In noneconomic terms, is the unanimous verdict requirement inefficient because it leaves one out of every twenty juries deadlocked? It has long been part of Anglo-American legal culture to treasure the hung jury "because it represents the legal system's respect for the minority viewpoint that is held strongly enough to thwart the will of the majority."[27] Living with deadlocks in every twentieth case hardly seems too high a price to pay for the hesitancy we ought to feel in the face of doubts so strongly held.

Abolishing the unanimous verdict would weaken the conversations through which laypersons educate one another about their common sense of justice.

The law and order attack on unanimous verdicts often assumes the old myth about hung juries—that one oddball, crank, or corrupt person can hang an entire jury. No doubt such a solitary, hanging jury does crop up now and again. But the central conclusion of Kalven and Zeisel's research on hung juries, confirmed many times since, is that one or two persons rarely hang juries in real life (only in movies such as Henry Fonda's *Twelve Angry Men*).[28]

If one or two persons manage to hold out in the end, they probably had company in the beginning. Thus, Kalven and Zeisel estimated that it takes a sizable minority faction on the first ballot—say, four or five persons—to produce the likelihood of a hung jury.[29] Such a factual finding takes much of the sting out of the conservative attack on the idiosyncratic or irrational behavior of hanging jurors. It turns out that we are dealing with a small subset of cases where a sizable number of jurors does entertain initial doubts about the majority view of the evidence. As Kalven and Zeisel put it in *The American Jury*, the primary cause of a hung jury is the "ambiguity of the case," not "an eccentric juror . . . refus[ing] to play his proper role."[30]

If conservatives exaggerate the gains from abolishing unanimous verdicts, liberals typically overstate the threats. Justice Douglas feared in his dissent in *Johnson* and *Apodaca* that attacks on the unanimous verdict would be followed by moves to abolish the presumption of innocence and the requirement of proof beyond a reasonable doubt.[31] All three of these procedural rights make the jury system slow to convict the guilty, and Douglas foresaw a rising "law and order" tide impatient with the inefficiency prized in the remark "Better to let 9 guilty persons go free than convict an innocent man."[32] But these worst-case scenarios have not been realized. In fact, over the last twenty years, no new state has accepted the Court's invitation to experiment with majority verdicts in felony cases. Politically, the unanimous verdict retains its appeal, very much a symbol of faith in the jury system.

The continuing popularity of the unanimous verdict is worthy of comment. One of the key functions of the criminal jury system is to le-

gitimize, in the eyes of the community, the state's use of its coercive powers. The jury gives legitimacy to an accused's imprisonment, even execu-
tion, because ordinary persons like ourselves give the verdict. But the
jury's ability to maintain public confidence in the administration of justice is fragile. It depends in part on drawing the jury from the community
at large so that all groups have a potential say in how justice is done. It
depends also on public confidence that jury verdicts are just, accurate,
and true. The strongest argument for retaining the unanimous verdict is
that it is central to the legitimacy of jury verdicts.[33]

Common sense alone tells us that public confidence in the accuracy
of verdicts is greater when the verdict is unanimous. Common sense also
tells us that Justice Potter Stewart was right to fret over the symbolic sig-
nificance of replacing unanimous verdicts with majority verdicts.[34] In the
best of circumstances, public confidence would erode whenever split verdicts resulted. In the worst cases, a crisis of legitimacy would greet verdicts
split along racial or other group lines. Justice Stewart did not cite statistics
about the probability of such group splits occurring. His point was that the
very redesign of jury trials to permit such verdicts changed public attitudes
toward the jury for the worst. It sponsored an ever present consciousness
that majorities, if large enough, could rule absolutely on juries.

In the end, however, it must be admitted that there is a paradox behind the unanimous verdict's contribution to the jury's legitimacy. Unanimity inspires confidence because the public *believes* that requiring all
jurors to agree promotes the search for truth. But, as Gary Jacobsohn
noted in his study of the unanimous verdict, this belief rests on at least a
partial misconception.[35] Unanimity might inspire jurors to behave delib-
eratively—that is, to reason together across differences to reach a genuinely shared verdict. But, as Justice Lewis Powell pointed out, unanimity
may prod jurors to behave more expediently, returning a compromise
verdict that splits the difference between jury factions and has no rational basis.[36] To the extent that this happens, unanimity does not promote
truth.[37]

But the public rarely learns of the compromises. The jury returns its
unanimous verdict and does not explain how the result was reached. As
far as the community is concerned, the unanimity reflects a genuine
meeting of the minds. It appears that the verdict must be right because all
jurors agreed it was right.

The analysis so far suggests that unanimous verdicts contribute to the
legitimacy of jury verdicts only so long as a certain fiction is maintained—that is, only so long as the public *mistakenly* believes that the
more consensual the verdict, the more likely the verdict is correct. But is
the public mistaken? Exactly how jurors "compromise" or harmonize
during deliberations remains a mystery; studies of mock jurors are not
likely to tell us how jurors behave when they bear actual responsibility for
the decision.

No doubt there are cases where jurors strike a bargain simply to agree
and go home, much like Justice Powell suggested. But jury compromises
need not be of the expedient, horse-trading, split-the-difference, or flip-a-
coin models.[38]

The alternative give-and-take model defines the democratic ideal of
deliberation. On this model, jurors do not strike compromises between

the different interests they represent. They each take seriously the goal of reaching the truth, earnestly seeking to harmonize their different understandings of the facts, their different assessments of an accused's culpability or responsibility for his acts. In the face of these differences, the conversation grows animated, intense, even angry. The unanimous verdict rule makes the deliberations all the more intense because the alternative of outshouting or outvoting opponents does not exist. In such circumstances, jurors certainly have incentives for compromising or harmonizing. But the cue we are giving jurors by requiring unanimity is that there are compromises and there are compromises. On the basic issue of whether an accused is guilty or not guilty, there can be no compromise, and even deadlocked jurors are carefully instructed that individual jurors should not "cave in" to achieve unanimity.

The whole point of having jurors deliberate face-to-face is to change people's preconceptions about a case through conversation with others. Unanimity empowers the conversation by signaling to jurors to put their opinions at risk. The ideal, which is often realized, is that power flows to the persuasive on the jury—that people change their minds not out of expediency but because their views actually have shifted through hearing the views of others. When deliberation works in this way, the achievement of unanimity speaks to the collection of wisdom, not the politics of compromise.

In Brazil, federal juries do not deliberate. At the close of evidence, jurors are individually polled in writing, a secret ballot is taken, and the majority prevails.[39] Such a procedure stands in stark contrast to our own, where deliberation is the essence of a juror's duty.

Replacing unanimous verdicts with majority verdicts would not obliterate deliberation altogether and import the Brazilian model. But it would alter the basic institutional design of our jury and the behavior promoted by that design. If they are instructed to return a unanimous verdict, jurors know their task is not to vote. For all their differences, they must approach justice through conversation and the art of persuading or being persuaded in turn. Majority verdicts signal an entirely different type of behavior, where jurors ultimately remain free to assert their different interests and opinions against one another. The distinctive genius of the jury system has been to emphasize deliberation more than voting and representation. Abolishing the unanimous verdict would weaken the conversations through which laypersons educate one another about their common sense of justice.

Notes

1. *Johnson v. Louisiana*, 406 U.S. at 374, n. 12 (opinion of Powell, J.) (1972).

2. Harry Kalven, Jr., and Hans Zeisel, *The American Jury* (Chicago: University of Chicago Press, 1970), pp. xv, 487, n. 12.

3. "Inside the Jury Room," "Frontline," April 11, 1986.

4. Kalven and Zeisel, *The American Jury*, p. 488 (emphasis omitted).

5. Ibid.

6. Ibid., pp. 460–61.

7. Jon M. Van Dyke, *Jury Selection Procedures: Our Uncertain Commitment to Representative Panels* (Cambridge, Mass.: Ballinger Publishing, 1977), p. 209.

8. Kalven and Zeisel, *The American Jury*, p. 460.

9. Jeffrey T. Frederick, *The Psychology of the American Jury* (Charlottesville, Va.: Michie Co., 1987), p. 283; Michael J. Saks, *Jury Verdicts: The Role of Group Size and Social Decision Rule* (Lexington, Mass.: Lexington Books, 1977), pp. 95–98; Charlan Nemeth, "Interactions Between Jurors as a Function of Majority vs. Unanimity Decision Rules," in *In the Jury Box: Controversies in the Courtroom*, ed. Lawrence S. Wrightsman, Saul M. Kassin, and Cynthia E. Willis (Beverly Hills, Calif.: Sage Publications, 1987), pp. 241, 246, 250, 253.

10. Reid Hastie, Steven D. Penrod, and Nancy Pennington, *Inside the Jury* (Cambridge, Mass.: Harvard University Press, 1983), p. 60; Saks, *Jury Verdicts*, p. 99; Nemeth, "Interactions Between Jurors," p. 241.

11. Nemeth, "Interactions Between Jurors," p. 250; Hastie et al., *Inside the Jury*, pp. 76, 90, 94–98; Lani Guinier, "Triumph of Tokenism: The Voting Rights Act and the Theory of Black Electoral Success," *Michigan Law Review* 89 (1991): 1122.

12. Hastie et al., *Inside the Jury*, pp. 94–98.

13. Saks, *Jury Verdicts*, p. 94.

14. Kalven and Zeisel, *The American Jury*, p. 460.

15. "The Supreme Court, 1971 Term," *Harvard Law Review* 86 (1972): 1, 153; Van Dyke, *Jury Selection Procedures*, p. 211.

16. Hastie et al., *Inside the Jury*, p. 60.

17. Ibid., pp. 88, 90.

18. Ibid., pp. 76–78; Nemeth, "Interactions Between Jurors," p. 244; Saks, *Jury Verdicts*, p. 95; John Guinther, *The Jury in America* (New York: Facts on File Publications, 1988), p. 83.

19. Hastie et al., *Inside the Jury*, p. 112.

20. Guinther, *Jury in America*, p. 81.

21. Ibid., p. 83.

22. Van Dyke, *Jury Selection Procedures*, p. 209.

23. For instance, under unanimous verdict rules, federal criminal juries convicted 82 percent of defendants in 1990. Bureau of Justice Statistics, U.S. Department of Justice, *Compendium of Federal Justice Statistics, 1990*, p. 31.

24. See n. 9.

25. Van Dyke, *Jury Selection Procedures*, p. 209.

26. Ibid.

27. Hans Zeisel, ". . . And Then There Were None: The Diminution of the Federal Jury," *University of Chicago Law Review* 38 (1971): p. 719, n. 42.

28. In the 1993 trial of three high school athletes from Glen Ridge, New Jersey, charged with raping a young, retarded woman, one juror initially held out from the decision of the eleven others to convict. Interviews after trial described how the eleven "went to work" on the lone holdout

who finally came into line. Jodi Enda, "Agonized Debate in Glen Ridge Case," *Philadelphia Inquirer*, March 18, 1993, p. S1. Similarly, in the 1994 trial of a Bucks County, Pennsylvania, woman for attempted murder, one juror held out for three days in favor of a not guilty by reason of insanity verdict. When she finally voted to convict, she said she was merely caving into pressure. She was "tired of being badgered, and she agreed to vote for a guilty verdict even though she had not changed her mind." Robert A. Farley, "Holdout Juror Said Pressure Was On," *Philadelphia Inquirer*, Jan. 13, 1994, p. A1.

29. Kalven and Zeisel, *The American Jury*, p. 462.

30. Ibid.

31. *Johnson v. Louisiana*, 406 U.S. at 392–94 (Douglas, J., dissenting).

32. Ibid. at 393.

33. See Gary C. Jacobsohn, "The Unanimous Verdict: Politics and the Jury Trial," *Washington Law Quarterly* 39 (1977): 48–57.

34. *Johnson v. Louisiana*, 406 U.S. at 397–99 (Stewart, J., dissenting).

35. Jacobsohn, "The Unanimous Verdict," p. 50.

36. *Johnson v. Louisiana*, 406 U.S. at 377 (opinion of Powell, J.).

37. In the celebrated Menendez brothers trials that ended in deadlocked juries for each brother in January 1994, some jurors told television interviewers that they had considered a compromise verdict between those voting manslaughter and those favoring a murder conviction on charges that the brothers had killed their parents. The compromise would have convicted the brothers of first-degree murder of their mother but only manslaughter in the slaying of the father, whom the brothers said abused them. No compromise was reached.

38. In February 1994 a jury rendered what was widely regarded as a compromise verdict in the trial of eleven Branch Davidians. The members were charged with murder in the notorious shootout that occurred when agents of the Federal Bureau of Alcohol, Tobacco and Firearms tried to serve a warrant on the group's compound in Waco, Texas, in 1993. The shootout left four agents and six Branch Davidians dead. At the outset of deliberations, according to one juror, "some thought it was outright murder on the part of the Branch Davidians. . . . [Others] thought it was outrageous murder on the part of the Federal Government." Eventually all jurors agreed that "there were a lot of dirty hands out there that day, on both sides." All twelve jurors agreed to acquit all Branch Davidians of murder charges but to convict seven of them on the lesser charge of voluntary manslaughter. According to the jury, murder was too harsh a sentence and the government bore some responsibility for its use of force. Sam Howe Verhovek, "Juror Says Doubts Determined Verdict in Sect Trial," *New York Times*, March 1, 1994, p. 21; Robert L. Jackson and Lianne Hart, "Waco Survivors' Trial to Open," *Philadelphia Inquirer*, Jan. 10, 1994, p. B3.

39. Herman G. James, *The Constitutional System of Brazil* (Washington, D.C.: Carnegie Institution of Washington, 1923), p. 122.

6

Peremptory Challenges Should Be Abolished

H. Lee Sarokin and G. Thomas Munsterman

H. Lee Sarokin, a judge for the U.S. District Court in New Jersey, formerly edited a column on trial techniques for the law journal Chambers to Chambers. *G. Thomas Munsterman is the director of the Center for Jury Studies at the National Center for State Courts in Arlington, Virginia. He has written extensively on the legal aspects of jury trials.*

Peremptory challenges allow lawyers to withdraw potential jurors during jury selection without giving a reason. This procedure enables lawyers to select juries that favor their clients. However, lawyers often base their decisions about when to use peremptory challenges on biased assumptions about race, gender, religion, and class. Such authorized bias is a form of institutionalized discrimination in the legal system that damages the ideals of fairness and justice. Abolishing peremptory challenges would minimize this bias during juror selection; it would also decrease trial length and expense while increasing public confidence in the judicial system.

The time may have come to consider the elimination of peremptory challenges, which permit a lawyer to excuse prospective jurors without providing a reason. There are many arguments for retaining these challenges, but current decisions may have furnished the catalyst to reexamine this practice and perhaps even to abandon it.

Recent rulings of the U.S. Supreme Court and appellate courts on the abuse of peremptory challenges recognize what trial judges and lawyers have always known—that discrimination in selecting jurors has been practiced systematically for decades, with the knowledge and acquiescence of the courts.[1] Lawyers use peremptory challenges to obtain a partial jury, not an impartial one. The fact that an impartial jury may result because challenges based upon bias offset each other does not alter the underlying rationale behind their use. Lawyers seek to exclude those potential jurors they believe will not find in their client's favor and to retain those who will. Their decisions are most often based on stereotypes and assumed prejudices.

If asked privately to articulate their reasons for excluding or not excluding certain jurors, attorneys will candidly say such things as "Jews and Italians are generous; bankers and engineers are not" or "persons of the same race, religion, or nationality as the party on trial are more likely to identify with, and thus rule for, that party." The myths abound, and advocacy guides have even been published codifying such supposed criteria.

Lawyers use peremptory challenges to obtain a partial jury, not an impartial one.

Under the recent Supreme Court decisions, in a growing number of cases, attorneys who appear to be engaged in discriminatory practices will be required to provide a nondiscriminatory justification for excusing certain classes of jurors.[2] We respectfully submit that this requirement will not end the objectionable practices but will merely compel lawyers to be more creative in finding reasons for excluding potential jurors. The only change will be the improved ingenuity of the attorneys who must justify their actions, and the court will be placed in the awkward and untenable position of judging the credibility and the good faith of trial lawyers.

The answer to the dilemma may be to consider abolishing peremptory challenges entirely, at least in civil cases.[3] This should be done not only as a matter of principle (because it will end this institutionalized condoning of discrimination in our judicial system) but as a practical consideration.[4] Three practical reasons for abolishing peremptory challenges are discussed below.

The case against challenges

First, an entire matter may be tried and decided, only to have an appellate court require a second trial because a peremptory challenge was improperly used before the trial began, rather than because of some substantial error during the trial. If discriminatory selection has been practiced, a new trial may be required.

Second, peremptory challenges are expensive and time-consuming. In federal court, at least sixteen jurors may be called and excused in criminal cases, and at least six in most civil cases. Many more may be challenged in multidefendant cases, both criminal and civil. Multiply that number in every court throughout the country by the number of trials, and the total of those peremptorily challenged and thus excluded from service is staggering. Each prospective juror must spend at least a day in court, be paid the required fee, and lose the equivalent amount of productive work time. This process involves thousands of people and millions of dollars each year.

Third, the strength of our judicial system is predicated and dependent on the public's confidence in the courts. That confidence is weakened when people are summoned to court, and, after having been required to leave their work and other responsibilities, excused without reason. Many may be relieved to be excused, but an equal number may be insulted, and justifiably so.[5]

What could be fairer than a group of jurors drawn by lot from a panel that represents a fair cross section of the community and subject only to valid challenges for cause? Many methods are used by the courts to try to ensure that the panel of prospective jurors is representative of the population (for example, reducing the term of service, using multiple source lists, eliminating exemptions from jury service, and making jury fees more realistic). But the demographic balance achieved through these efforts can be easily destroyed by only a few discriminatory peremptory challenges. It is evident that no one can predict how a juror will decide a particular case, and participants in our judicial system should not be permitted to do so when those predictions are based upon unfounded assumptions of bias or prejudice.[6]

No more bias

In the search for a fair and impartial jury, the means for attaining it should not be tainted by assumption of bias or prejudice based solely upon race, nationality, gender, religion, or occupation, even if the attributed characteristic is favorable rather than unfavorable. A bias is still a bias, even where tendered in the form of a compliment. Recognizing that there are valid arguments for retaining peremptory challenges, at a minimum we strongly recommend that the idea of abandoning them be considered and that it be supported by study and an open dialogue. This would allow both for determining whether or not peremptory challenges should survive, and for deciding what changes in voir dire [the process of jury selection] and challenges for cause might be required.

Notes

1. *Kentucky v. Batson*, 476 U.S. 79 (1986); *Edmonson v. Leesville Concrete Co. Inc.*, 111 S.Ct. 2077 (1991); *Hernandez v. New York*, 111 S.Ct. 1859 (1991); *Powers v. Ohio*, 111 S.Ct. 1364 (1991); *Georgia v. McCollum*, 91-372 (decided June 18, 1992); and *U.S. v. DeGross*, 960 F.2d 1433 (1992).

2. *Kentucky v. Batson* at 17.

3. Civil jury trials are used in England (Queens Bench) only for libel, slander, malicious prosecution, and false imprisonment, and there is no right to peremptory challenges in such cases. *Halsbury's Laws of England*, vol. 26, 4th ed (London: Butter-Worths, 1979), para 624.

4. If the use of experts continues and expands, it will give the litigant another advantage (through the exercise of peremptory challenges)—assuming such experts can predict any juror's vote.

5. Albert W. Alschuler, "The Supreme Court and Jury: Voir Dire, Peremptory Challenges, and the Review of Jury Verdicts," *University of Chicago Law Review*, vol. 56 (Winter 1989), pp. 153–233.

6. True, there will be the occasional juror whose presence on the jury troubles an attorney for reasons that cannot be determined or articulated. But Judge Sarokin, who regularly meets with jurors in his chambers after trial, is constantly amazed and uplifted by their conscientiousness and dedication to their duties. Furthermore, every lawyer has an anecdote about a juror who, it was certain, would decide one way but in fact did just the opposite.

7

Peremptory Challenges Should Be Retained

Raymond Brown

Raymond Brown is a criminal-defense lawyer in Newark, New Jersey. In addition, he is the director of the National Association of Criminal Defense Lawyers and a fellow of the American College of Trial Lawyers.

The peremptory challenge—the practice that allows a lawyer to exclude prospective jurors from a trial without providing a reason—is an effective legal device that should be retained. Critics maintain that peremptory challenges have been used to exclude individuals of a particular race, gender, or class from juries. However, peremptory challenges have also been used to ensure that some jurors will be of the same ethnicity or gender as the defendant or will have a mindset sympathetic toward the defendant. If peremptory challenges are abolished, defendants from minority groups are more likely to be tried by juries composed solely of majority members and therefore may face significant discrimination.

Editor's Note: The following viewpoint was originally a speech presented to the American Criminal Law Review's *symposium at the Georgetown University Law Center on March 5, 1994.*

By an ideologically neutral process, I have been selected as the bête noire [detested person] of this symposium. I accept that challenge and, whatever your reaction, I will always love you.[1]

After the Rodney King verdict,[2] I was appointed to a New Jersey Supreme Court committee[3] charged with making recommendations about jury selection in New Jersey. The group included a cross-section of the legal community. When the committee debated these issues, it eventually reached the issue of peremptory challenges; the dividing line in the committee was fascinating. It was not left vs. right; it was not black vs. white; it was not male vs. female; it was not heterosexual vs. homosexual. There were trial lawyers on one side, and judges and academics on the other. Under the "strange bedfellows" test, I am not sure which of those two latter groups should be more concerned or horrified.

Criminal defense lawyers, prosecutors, and civil lawyers for both plaintiff and defense were unanimous in their opposition to losing the peremptory challenge because it is necessary to effectively represent their clients. Obviously, one could raise the criticism that this is merely the wailing and crying of a group afraid of being deprived of its favorite toy. Consequently, we need to take a much deeper look to see whether there is any legitimacy to the almost universal claim by those "in the pits" every day that the peremptory challenge is an important tool to protect litigants at trial.

Hurting minorities

My approach is simply that of a trial lawyer. I am not a scholar. I am not an intellectual, so I will not engage in the admirable and fancy intellectual footwork that has gone on since the decision in *Batson v. Kentucky*.[4] [In the 1986 case of *Batson v. Kentucky*, the Supreme Court ruled that prosecutors could no longer exercise race-based peremptory challenges.] I am, however, someone who deals with these issues on a day-to-day basis and who also has, as ideological baggage, a concern about what happens in our criminal courts and who is being tried there.

There are really two things we need to analyze to get to the bottom of this debate and to test the practitioners' claim. I think we must first consider how we treat the least fortunate, the pariahs in our society. I imagine you will accept that the treatment of those defendants who are least popular and most likely to be hated or despised is a test of the effectiveness of the system. How does the system work for them?

Second, I assume you are willing to question whether the *Batson* analysis is an honest one. Is there any such thing as a racially neutral "anything" in America, or is that a ruse and an invitation to hypocrisy? Ultimately, I think you will be forced to the conclusion that the group being injured includes young blacks, Chicanos and Latinos, the usual pariahs who nobody wants and to whom we are being absolutely dishonest in our analysis. As a result, I believe the only solution is to eviscerate *Batson*, and focus our social engineering on changing the jury venire [jury pool] and stopping the pretense that somehow we can elevate the mythical right of jurors over that of defendants. Talk about living in an unreal world!

What do W.E.B. DuBois and Hans Christian Andersen have in common? DuBois tells us that race is the dominant question of the 20th century,[5] and Hans Christian Andersen tells us of the little child who stood at the parade and was the only one willing to say "the emperor has no clothes."[6]

Candor and honesty require us to admit there is not a decision that we make in terms of social grouping that does not involve an analysis of race, a quick look at gender, and perhaps a glance at sexual orientation— a look at the very factors that we are now sweeping under the rug. In this regard, I suggest that you think about something that has been a significant experience in my life. For the past twenty years, I have been talking to black kids in high schools and colleges about black history, because blacks know too little of our[7] history. The question that I have posed to every high school and college group to whom I have spoken is a simple one: What was the principal issue facing civil rights groups at the beginning of World War II? To this day, after speaking to thousands of students, not one has answered the question correctly. The answer is "lynching." Lynching was the issue that preoccupied the African-American community at the beginning of World War II.[8]

Blacks are still being lynched in large numbers. I suggest it as a troublesome metaphor because carried to its ultimate and logical conclusion, concern about the community's attitude about the pariah is toleration of the lynch mob. That is not to suggest that the Supreme Court is a lynch mob, but to suggest that at one end of that extreme exists some very, very dangerous territory.[9]

I find that popular culture is always a good way for me to get insight into deep questions because, although there has been a lot of fancy intellectual sleight-of-hand, I feel the need to put the fodder where the lambs can reach it. I recall not long ago—and I take some risk in telling you this story because it reveals some of my own sexism, which I am still in the process of trying to eradicate with much help from Wanda, who is my love—my sixteen-year-old daughter overheard me say to a friend that I hoped that her first sexual experience would be in her second marriage. She was horrified and took me to see a movie called "Father of the Bride" for punishment and rehabilitation. So I began to see there is pedagogical value in popular culture.

Last January [1993], I was listening to National Public Radio and a commentator said that for the first time in the history of America, the top twenty musical hits on the charts were all by non-white groups. Look at the fact that the young people of America are listening to music predominantly by non-white groups.[10] Furthermore, one week, all of the top twenty songs were by non-white groups, and the top song was "I Will Always Love You," a Whitney Houston "cover" of a Dolly Parton song. This clearly reflects a reversal in the normal dynamics of our culture. What does that mean? What does that have to do with *Batson*?

There is a profound change taking place in America. If you are thoughtful and care about the future, if you sit somewhere in an ivory tower or in a court where your job is to pontificate about these questions, you have to think about the future and look at the last two census counts and see that the only group in America whose percentage in the population has not changed are those people we insensitively call "white people."

The treatment of those defendants who are least popular and most likely to be hated or despised is a test of the effectiveness of the system.

By the middle of the next century, more than half of all Americans will claim their place of origin from some place other than western Europe. By the middle of the next century, there will be more Muslims than Jews in America. Two months ago [January 1994] a man was mugged in New Jersey by a Vietnamese gang. This would have been unthinkable when I was a child—not a mugging, but a Vietnamese gang in New Jersey. These are profound changes, and they do not even begin to deal with the less empirically verifiable changes relating to the role of women in

American society, and our acceptance or nonacceptance of homosexual activity and different kinds of cultures. (Of course, if you listen to Pat Buchanan you know the response to that.)

These profound changes affect the Court. As Professor [Nancy] King suggests when she talks about *Shaw v. Reno*,[11] [the Supreme Court case that concluded that voters could challenge the legality of racially gerrymandered voting districts] the Court is engaging in a bit of social engineering (we like it when it goes our way; we all object to it when it goes the wrong way). The democratic institution the Court unfortunately chose to tinker with is not jury selection as a whole or even the venire [jury selection] process, which could use some tinkering, but the peremptory challenge.

This tinkering, done in the name of an amorphous right to jury service, subordinates the defendant's rights to some perceived need of the community. Talk about Hans Christian Andersen! How many people get that little slip about jury service and say, "Please judge, let me serve an extra term?" What they really do is call you and say, "If you're worth your salt as a lawyer, you will get me out of jury service."

The reality is not a public clamoring to be on juries, but a fiction designed to cure another problem. That problem is the real concern of the Court: What is going to happen to the new racial mix of America, and how will that affect the integrity and the perception of the jury system in the future? Therefore, the Court begins to tinker, but it tinkers in a very dangerous way and in a very dangerous area, and it is not always honest about its tinkering.

A policy debate about race

Back at the time when I was debating with my friends about Clarence Thomas' Supreme Court nomination (there were one or two people to whom I was still speaking who favored his nomination), I tried to suggest to them my "strange bedfellows" test: If you are in bed with Strom Thurmond [the Republican senator from South Carolina who supported Thomas' nomination] you ought to be worried, and therefore you should agree with me.

Since then I have abandoned the "strange bedfellows" test because I am now in bed with Justice [Antonin] Scalia and Justice Thomas, and am opposed to Justice [Thurgood] Marshall and Justice [Harry] Blackmun on the *Batson* issue. I am in the middle of this mix because the Justices to whom Americans have been turning for racial sensitivity, and perhaps even sensitivity to the rights of criminal defendants, are off on a crusade. They have tried to communicate that "I will always love you" and they are doing it through the peremptory challenge.

I suggest that there are three passages that are worth examining to clarify this debate. One is Justice [Lewis] Powell's opinion in *Batson*: "*In view of the heterogeneous population of our Nation*, public respect for our criminal justice system and the rule of law will be strengthened if we ensure that no citizen is disqualified from jury service because of his race."[12] This foreshadows the tortured logic of Justice [Anthony] Kennedy, but does not really address jury selection or peremptory challenges. Rather, it raises the policy question of a changing America. It is not about the dy-

namics of trial, about which nobody has thought or seems to care. That
is a bit strong, but it certainly leads us in the right direction.

On the other side, Justice Scalia, who is always a rather pointed fellow, talks in *Georgia v. McCollum*[13] [the 1992 case in which the Supreme
Court prohibited defense lawyers from exercising race-based peremptory
challenges] about the real issues being considered:

> In the interest of promoting *the supposedly greater good of race rela-
> tions in a society as a whole (make no mistake that that is what under-
> lies* all of this) we use the Constitution to destroy the ages-old right
> of criminal defendants to exercise peremptory challenges as they
> wish to secure a jury they consider fair. I dissent.[14]

What is most important about the dissent is that Justice Scalia is pulling
the covers off the debate and effectively saying, "Look, what you're really
talking about is some higher good. You're not concerned about the dynamics of this delicate thing called a trial. You're not concerned about the
black criminal defendant in Bergen County, New Jersey, who is going to
get a trial in front of a jury where there may be two blacks in the whole
venire, and the lawyer may have to use racially conscious strikes to get
one of them on the jury. You are not concerned about that."[15]

Finally, there is Justice Blackmun—a man I have grown to admire
more and more as time goes on—who wrote (in an unrelated case dealing
with a hate crime statute):

> [I]n the second instance is the possibility that this case will not sig-
> nificantly alter First Amendment jurisprudence, but, instead, will
> be regarded as an aberration—a case where the Court manipulated
> doctrine to strike down an ordinance whose premise it opposed,
> namely, that racial threats and verbal assaults are of greater harm
> than other fighting words. *I fear that the Court has been distracted
> from its proper mission by the temptation to decide the issue over "polit-
> ically correct speech" and "cultural diversity," neither of which is pre-
> sented here.* If this is the meaning of today's opinion, it is perhaps
> even more regrettable.[16]

Interestingly enough, Justice Blackmun wrote this opinion four days after
Justice Scalia wrote his dissent in *McCollum*. Justice Blackmun's opinion
dramatizes the policy issue here.

Unfortunately, what we have is a policy debate about race, a profoundly important question that may go to the heart of the survival of
this republic, taking place on the metaphorical field of the peremptory
challenge. Ironically, the peremptory is one of the few tools we have to
try to right the imbalance faced by a defendant who is unpopular, who
nobody likes, who jurors start out hating because of the color of his skin,
or because of some other thing over which that person has no control.
We must be concerned about whether all these very important intellectual policy debates are upsetting an apple cart that was delicately balanced in the beginning. We also have to ask ourselves if *Batson* is a Mag-
inot Line [a system of defensive barricades that fails to prevent enemy
invasion] we are constructing against this evil of racism while ignoring an
enemy invasion of the jury system.

Am I the only person in America who looks at political campaigns and
realizes that the first step in planning a campaign is to find out where the
black folks live, where the Chicanos live, where there are many people in

households with incomes of a certain amount, and where there are single mothers raising children and, only then, on the basis of these findings, do you formulate policy and strategy? Am I the only one who recognizes that only when the chips are really down, and we are talking about whether we are going to steal money for the B-1 bomber or give it to Head Start, that demographic issues get talked about? Of course these are real issues, and they are infinitely more complex than saying, "She's black so she should go," but you must start there and not ignore that reality.

Defendants deserve sympathetic juries

Then, of course, there are the administrative problems of *Batson*. Professor [Deborah] Ramirez's ideas constitute interesting variations on the jury system. They are worth talking about and they are worth examining. [Professor Ramirez argues that lawyers should be able to actively select jurors, not just peremptorily exclude jurors.] However, my experience suggests that the general quality of the judiciary is not what you expect once you emerge into the real world and find the judiciary uninterested in debates about *Pennoyer*[17] [*v. Neff*] or the refined points of the Constitution.

In fact, if you go into state courts, they do not want to know about the Supreme Court. In New Jersey, the state supreme court's reporters are a distinctive shade of vanilla yellow. One does not bring reporters containing Third Circuit or Supreme Court opinions into court.

You will find that many judges are there not because they are known for sagacity and wisdom, but because they had bad backs and could not get to any other practice or they have some relationship with someone important. This is the truth, and if we're going to have candor, let's have candor. There ought not to be an intellectual test for the judiciary, because the question of intellect leaves out the question of character.

Therefore, though the case suggests otherwise, *Batson*'s complex requirement for establishing a prima facie [self-evident] case of race based challenges, theoretically involving statistics, voir dire [jury selection], and questions and comments of counsel, is reduced to: "Mr. Brown, you've just excused three Asians in a row. That is obviously a prima facie case."

Most judges have a bright-line test of three, four, or seven people of a cognizable group. Once the magic number is reached, a prima facie case is established and then you are tempted to engage in that thing which is absolutely horrible: lying in a courtroom.[18] You have an ethical duty to be candid to the court, and yet we all know that pretext is the name of the game here. The courts do not recognize the pretext because, of course, we are back to Hans Christian Andersen! They have to pretend it really is not going on and yet it is the critical issue in most of the personal and social decisions we make in our lives. This myth of color blindness is leading us into a place where the consequences are terrible.

I mentioned Bergen County, and those of you not from New Jersey will not know what it means, but there is a string of roads that goes up Interstate 95, and one of the important links is called the New Jersey Turnpike. Several empirical studies have shown that, if you are black and you drive on the Turnpike, your chances of being stopped by the constabulary are infinitely increased. If they happen to stop you in Hunterdon County or they happen to stop you in Bergen County, where very few blacks live, you are going to be tried in a venue where the jury pool contains nobody who even remotely looks like you or likes you. That is a profound problem. It is a serious, serious problem for the Supreme Court to take away challenges so that, when choosing from people who are alien in culture and ideas, your chance to select those who might be more favorable to you or who might be less prejudiced against you is reduced.

There also must be some real changes in terms of voir dire. Voir dire tends, especially when it is judicially administered, to be a hollow mockery. "Are you going to be prejudiced against this snot-nosed defendant over here or are you going to give him a fair trial?" Then for that potential juror who was asleep and gave the wrong answer, there is what I call the Lazarus syndrome. You rehabilitate that juror by saying, "When you said you would be *unfair* you really thought I meant *fair* because you didn't hear me very well because the acoustics in the room were temporarily bad."

This process goes on because there is an emphasis in the administrative apparatus of the state and federal courts on moving cases. It involves a quantitative assessment of justice. In most of the vicinages in America, judges are evaluated not on the Solomonic content of their opinions, but on how many cases they move. If you take too much time, especially in jury selection—"Because you know counsel, I could take the first twelve people and try this case"—then you have offended that sense of progress required by a public understandably frightened by crime.

The peremptory is one of the few tools we have to try to right the imbalance faced by a defendant who . . . jurors start out hating because of the color of his skin.

Opponents of the unbridled peremptory challenge cite Justice Marshall's opposition to it as support for their opposition.[19] The problem with using Justice Marshall in this way is that his analysis was a historical one. Justice Marshall, who litigated cases in the South, was the conscience of this country with respect to the judicial system as it affected litigation in the South at a time when blacks were overtly excluded from the entire franchise. It is not surprising that a person with that kind of historical legacy is going to criticize anything that is a potential tool for discrimination.

I have had potential jurors say to me in Union County, New Jersey during voir dire: "I don't like blacks." One day it happened and my co-counsel said, "That juror is really honest—we should keep him." I said, "Are you out of your mind? Jurors do not get points for candor." But the fact of the matter is that a searching voir dire can elicit much, and can ultimately create something which I suspect all of you embrace even if you embrace nothing else.

In the last analysis, I do not want a jury of blacks to judge my black defendant. I want a jury who likes me, is going to like him and then render a verdict of not guilty at the end. Therefore, if you let me know more about those assembled individuals, about their kids and their grandparents, about their ideas, feelings, thoughts and nuances, then I am less likely to stereotype them as women, blacks or other labels with which we work, which have some basis in reality, but in practice distort our perceptions. As a defense attorney, I can begin to focus on real things, on real feelings about the nature of the trial, and then begin to participate in the process that may have a racial element and a gender component.

For example, one of the experiences I have had in twenty years of trying cases is that women are stronger than men. If I have a choice between women jurors who I think will go my way and men, I want the women. My experience has been that almost every hung jury I have had involved one or two women, usually of good size, who sat in the corner, folded their arms and said, "I am not convicting this defendant." I cannot explain those dynamics. Women are superior to men in many contexts and so I want to make gender-based decisions.[20] The fact of the matter is that gender and race and all of these things we pretend to eschew lie at the heart of all of the political and social decisions we make in our lives.

While many aspects of the jury system horrify me, if or when they indict me, I want to be tried in America by a jury. I have seen a few verdicts that went the way I did not like them to go, especially—and I know you should not admit this in a symposium—when I lost a case. However, I very seldom come away feeling that the jurors were not serious. I very seldom come away feeling that the jurors totally disregarded their duty. It is an amazing system, infinitely preferable to one judge sitting and making the judgment, subject to all the political pressures that may force him to take that bad back out and actually earn a living.

When we tinker with how the system functions, we tinker with it at our peril. Yes, there are things that have to be done. There are jury selection and venue questions that have not been examined hard. The judge who sent the first Rodney King trial to Simi Valley said, in effect, "I do not believe black and Latino jurors will give these white cops a fair trial. I do not believe in the minority members of our community." That is troublesome to me. We must talk about judicial attitudes and the very complex, but important questions about how venue is selected and how the venire can be broadened. Can we comb the welfare rolls to make sure there is economic and racial disparity among the venire? There are some federal limitations on the use of public assistance information to inform and affect the way in which a venire is chosen.

Peremptory challenges are necessary

There are all kinds of things we can do if we are genuinely concerned about expressing to this entire polyglot republic, "I will always love you." However, we cannot do it by taking away something important from the people who need it most; the ability to say, "I grew up in this town and I know what bigotry is and I know how that guy over there with the blue tie feels about us, not about the facts of my case, but about us." I want a shot to be judged by those who are at least going to look at me and see my humanity.

The important policy debates that have led the Supreme Court to the mistaken application of important doctrines have taken us down a very dangerous road. Both sides of the Court—Justices Thomas, [Sandra Day] O'Connor, Marshall, and Scalia, and Chief Justices [Warren] Burger and [William] Rehnquist—have predicted[21] the thing about which trial lawyers have been screaming—that abolition of the peremptory challenge lies at the end of this road. To take away that tool, especially from that most benighted soul—the unpopular criminal defendant who is black, who is Latino, who is a pariah—is, in and of itself, a criminal and amoral act. I hope in some way this essay has discharged the responsibility that I accepted as "bête noire," and I will always love you.

Notes

1. This essay is based on a speech presented to the *American Criminal Law Review*'s symposium "Race, Gender, Juries and Justice," at the George-town University Law Center, March 5, 1994. No attempt has been made to correct "anomalies" that emerge when producing a written text from the spoken word.

2. The reference is to the April 29, 1992 verdict in the trial of *California v. Powell*. Four police officers were acquitted of assault charges in connection with their videotaped arrest and beating of black motorist Rodney King. The matter received great attention in both electronic and print media. My views on that trial were expressed in Raymond Brown, *It's Just Not Right: Reflections on Rodney King and His Case*, CHAMPION, July 1992.

3. New Jersey Supreme Court Ad Hoc Committee on Jury Selection.

4. 476 U.S. 79 (1986).

5. "*The problem of the twentieth century is the problem of the color line*, the question as to how far differences of race—which show themselves chiefly in the color of the skin and the texture of the hair—will hereafter be made the basis of denying to over half the world the right of sharing to their utmost ability the opportunities and privileges of modern civilization." W.E.B. DuBois, Address to the Nations of the World, First Pan-African Conference, London (1900) (emphasis added).

6. HANS CHRISTIAN ANDERSEN, THE EMPEROR'S NEW CLOTHES (1837).

7. The speaker-author is an African-American male.

8. *See* ROBERT ZANGARO, THE NAACP CRUSADE AGAINST LYNCHING, 1909–1950 (1980). A definitive work on the subject remains IDA WELLS BARNETT, ON LYNCHINGS (1969), a volume containing her pamphlets written in the 1890's. Also of historical interest is WALTER WHITE, ROPE AND FAGGOT, A BIOGRAPHY OF JUDGE LYNCH (1929) and CLARENCE NORRIS, THE LAST OF THE SCOTTSBORO BOYS (1979). (Clarence Norris is the last surviving defendant from Powell v. Alabama, 287 U.S. 45 (1932).) The most recent work on this famous case is JAMES GOODMAN, STORIES OF SCOTTSBORO (1994). Those under the impression that lynch law was a purely racial affair are directed to Frank v. Mangum, 237 U.S. 309 (1915) and ROBERT FREY & NANCY FREY, THE SILENT AND THE DAMNED, THE MURDER OF MARY PHAGAN AND THE LYNCHING OF LEO FRANK (1988).

9. In Powers v. Ohio, 499 U.S. 400 (1991), Justice Anthony Kennedy tortures the Equal Protection Clause to derive a third party standing argument permitting a litigant (in *Powers*, a criminal defendant) to raise the claims of jurors improperly excluded from service. This legal sophistry is compounded by the assertion that the right of jurors to serve is justified by Alexis De Tocqueville's view that juror service reflects the "magistery" of democracy. Little thought is given to the reality that some of those anxious for jury service resemble vigilantes more than magistrates.

10. On reviewing a draft of this speech, my friend and colleague Alan Dexter Bowman, who disagrees with my views on *Batson*, reminded me that "Black music is the soundtrack of American life."

11. 113 S. Ct. 2816 (1993).

12. *Batson*, 476 U.S. at 99 (emphasis added).

13. 112 S. Ct. 2348 (1992).

14. 112 S. Ct. at 2365 (Scalia, J., dissenting) (emphasis added).

15. In a sarcastic aside, the *New Republic* noted that "Rehnquist, Scalia and Thomas have managed to restrain their concern for black criminal defendants on most other occasions." Jeff Rosen, *Jurymandering: A Case Against Peremptory Challenges*, NEW REPUBLIC, Nov. 30, 1992, at 15. Well, my "strange bedfellows" test has to be thrown out.

16. R.A.V. v. City of St. Paul, 112 S. Ct. 2538, 2560 (1992) (Blackmun, J., concurring in the judgment) (emphasis added).

17. Pennoyer v. Neff, 95 U.S. 714 (1877).

18. *See, e.g.*, MODEL RULES OF PROFESSIONAL CONDUCT Rule 3.3 (1983).

19. See Justice Marshall's concurring opinion in *Batson*, 476 U.S. at 102.

20. This speech was delivered prior to the Supreme Court's ruling in J.E.B. v. Alabama *ex rel.* T.B., 114 S. Ct. 1419 (1994).

21. A few of the Cassandra-like predictions include: "The decision today will not end the racial discrimination that peremptories inject into the jury-selection process. That goal can be accomplished only by eliminating peremptory challenges entirely." *Batson*, 476 U.S. at 102–03 (Marshall, J., concurring). "[I]f conventional equal protection principles apply, then presumably defendants could object to exclusions on the basis of not only race, but also sex, age, religious or political affiliation, mental capacity, number of children, living arrangements, and employment in a particular industry, or profession." *Batson*, 476 U.S. at 124 (Burger, C.J., Rehnquist, J., dissenting) (citations omitted). "I am certain that black criminal defendants will rue the day that this court ventured down this road that inexorably will lead to the elimination of peremptory strikes." *McCollum*, 112 S. Ct. at 2359 (Thomas, J., concurring in the judgment).

8

Juries Should Be Informed of Their Right to Nullify the Law

Larry Dodge

Larry Dodge is the cofounder of the Fully Informed Jury Association in Helmville, Montana.

Throughout U.S. history, juries have had the right to express their disapproval of unreasonable laws by acquitting guilty defendants. This practice, known as jury nullification, was intended as a way for citizens to check and balance the power of the government. However, since 1895, when the Supreme Court ruled that judges were not required to inform juries of this veto power, jury nullification has seldom occurred. Because they are not told about their nullification power, many jurors mistakenly believe they must apply laws that they consider unjust or convict defendants who had valid reasons for breaking the law. Jurors should be routinely informed of their right to vote their conscience in order to prevent such miscarriages of justice.

April 7, 1988 was a very bad day for Darlene and Jerry Span, sibling owner-operators of a flea market in their yard in Phoenix, Arizona. The trouble began when two casually dressed men entered the market to show them a photo of a man they said was a fugitive from justice and, furthermore, that it was a photo of their brother Mickey Michael. They then demanded that the Spans produce him.

The Spans looked at the photo, remarking that it in no way resembled their brother, that the name on the photo was not spelled like their brother's, and that besides, Mickey Michael was not on the premises. Jerry said he didn't know the man in the picture, but would show it around to see if anyone else did. Then he and his sister made their first mistake: they turned their backs on the two men, to attend some of their customers.

At that time, according to witnesses, one of the men grabbed Darlene by the hair and flung her to the ground, while the other hit Jerry in the

"Fully Informed Juries—the Secret Silver Bullet?" by Larry Dodge. Paper (1994) from a Fully Informed Jury Association information packet. Reprinted with permission of the author.

head, kicked him in the back, shoved him to the ground and held him there—no difficult task, since he outweighed Jerry by about 90 pounds. As one witness later put it, the Spans ". . . had their backs turned when [the two men] blind-sided them. Darlene and Jerry never knew what hit them."

The Spans' mother, Virginia, upon hearing the commotion, got out of bed, where she had been recuperating after hospitalization, and worked her way downstairs to see what the trouble was. She had the presence of mind to bring a camera, and began snapping photos of the assault, whereupon the heavier of the two men grabbed her, wrested the camera away, opened it, tore out the film, and squashed it with his heel.

Jerry and Darlene, fearful for their mother's safety, then made their second mistake: they tried to come to her rescue, but were beaten back and prevented from reaching her. Someone called the Phoenix police, and when they arrived on the scene, the two men finally identified themselves as federal marshals David Dains and Garry Grotewold. Jerry and Darlene were then arrested and charged with assaulting federal officers in their course of duty.

Perhaps their third mistake was this: they asked for a trial by jury. The Spans figured their case was solid. There were witnesses, and some other photos that the marshals hadn't been able to destroy; the men had not identified themselves as law officers before attacking them; and the Span family had been longtime local residents with spotless records and a reputation for hard work and honest business dealings. Surely, a jury would exonerate them.

A miscarriage of justice

But Jerry and Darlene simply weren't prepared for the way the justice system works in this day and age. They didn't know that some of their best witnesses would be intimidated into leaving town, or that their lawyer would do a half-hearted job for them. They didn't anticipate that an affidavit from another federal marshal alleging that Dains and Grotewold had a track record of provoking violence would not be allowed into evidence, or that the marshals would lie under oath (Dains, for example, claimed that Virginia had bitten him—and the jury was never told that she had no teeth!). They didn't realize that there would be no way to tell the jury how the marshals had beaten up their father Bill at his home prior to arriving at the market—after all, there were no witnesses to that beating.

Most seriously, the Spans did not realize that the jury would be instructed by federal Judge Robert Broomfield that they were to apply the letter of the law as he gave it to them, whether or not they agreed with the law. His interpretation of the law was this: "Federal officers engaged in good faith and colorable performance of their duties may not be forcibly resisted, even if the resister turns out to be correct, that the resisted actions should not, in fact, have been taken. The statute requires him to submit peaceably and seek legal redress thereafter."

Thus instructed, the jury returned guilty verdicts, then surrounded and embraced Jerry and Darlene, several of them in tears. They explained that they saw through the whole charade, and believed the Spans were really in the right, but felt they "had no choice but to convict" because of what the judge said. Five of them later filed an affidavit with the court expressing their remorse at being forced to apply such an unjust statute. In their own words, "Such a law is completely unfair and against everything that the United States stands for."

Alas, it was to no avail. The Span case is still festering in the federal appeals courts. Untold tens of thousands of dollars have been invested in their defense, their business is gone, and both their parents have since died—Bill apparently having never recovered from his beating. And yes, it did turn out that Mickey Michael Span was not the man that Dains and Grotewold were looking for, after all. [In February 1996, a federal appeals court overturned the Spans' convictions because of faulty evidence.]

Is this an isolated incident? Hardly. Does it sound a lot like what happened to the Branch Davidians, in Waco, Texas? Does the arrest methodology recall what happened to Randy Weaver, in Ruby Creek, Idaho? Does the remorse expressed by the jury remind us of how the jurors felt after convicting the defendants in the famous Sanctuary Cases—of violating immigration laws by harboring refugees from Central America who would have been killed had they not fled to the United States?

And these well-known cases are just the tip of the iceberg. There were many cases during the 1960s and 70s in which juries tearfully convicted young men who resisted the draft because they, like the defendants, felt that the Viet Nam war was immoral. Our penitentiaries contain untold numbers of battered women who, after years of beatings, intimidation, and failed escape attempts, finally killed their abusive husbands. Most were convicted of first degree murder by juries told they had to follow "the letter of the law."

History's secret: jury veto power

America now leads the world in the percent of its population behind bars, and a substantial fraction of these inmates (as high as half of them, by the estimate of at least one state penitentiary warden known to this author) are "harmless." Many of them indeed violated the letter of the law, but had good moral reasons for doing so—reasons which either cut no ice with the judge, or were not considered by juries because the judge would not allow it.

Unfortunately, the escalating incarceration rate is used by government to document an alleged "crime wave," which in turn allows its agents to violate still more individual rights and to disinform still more juries. This "justifies" the passage of still more restrictive laws, construction of still more prisons, and incarceration of still more citizens, both harmless and otherwise, in an ever-accelerating vicious cycle.

It wasn't always so. There was once a mechanism by which the citizens could control their government—could say "no" to bad law (or the misapplication of good law), thus ensuring that prison time was rarely served by those whose actions were not harmful to society. That mechanism was called "jury veto power," or "jury nullification of law." It remains in force today, but only as the best-kept secret of the justice system, a secret which desperately needs telling if the juggernaut of neo-fascism is to be stopped.

What is it? Simply put, jury nullification is the power of the jury to judge the law itself, as well as the evidence, in deciding a verdict. It would have made all the difference in the Span case, for example, had the jurors known that the law they detested was "on trial," as much as Jerry and Darlene. If their own sense of justice would not allow them, in good conscience, to find the Spans guilty, they could have acquitted them, despite the "letter of the law" and the evidence given them.

But they didn't know they had such power, because they were not told about it, and not to know it is not to have it. In fact, it's been a century since juries have been routinely reminded by the courts of their power to reach a verdict according to conscience, the law and facts of the case notwithstanding. It used to be normal procedure for the judge to tell the jury that the law was a guideline, not a mandate, for its deliberations. But ever since a bitterly split Supreme Court decision in 1895 (*Sparf and Hansen v. US*), which held that it is not "reversible error" for the judge to fail to so inform the jurors, the bench has largely gone mum on the subject.

It used to be normal procedure for the judge to tell the jury that the law was a guideline, not a mandate, for its deliberations.

This century of silence represents perhaps the most serious—if unsung—usurpation of citizen power since the nation's Founders wrote and ratified our Constitution and Bill of Rights. The Framers were well aware of the power of juries to buffer government power and thwart government tyranny, and therefore included the right of trial by jury no less than three times in their handiwork—once in the main body of the Constitution, and twice in the Bill of Rights, as Amendments 6 and 7 (and once more, by implication, in the "due process" portion of Amendment 5).

Their perspective is nicely summarized by Thomas Jefferson in a 1789 letter to Thomas Paine, in which he said, "I consider trial by jury as the only anchor yet devised by man, by which a government can be held to the principles of its constitution."

The reason the Founders were so enamored of the principle of trial by jury, borrowed directly from English common law, was hard experience. They knew that colonist William Penn had been freed of charges that he had preached an illegal religion (Quakerism) in London in 1670, by jurors who had stood their ground for acquittal despite being detained without food, water, or toilet facilities for days. All were then fined for delivering a not guilty verdict, and four were imprisoned for refusing to pay the fine. Their release by the highest court of England established not only that jurors have the power to find the verdict as they see fit, with impunity, but also established our freedoms of speech, peaceable assembly, and religion.

The Founders were doubtless aware that the witch trials in Salem had finally ceased following fifty-two jury acquittals. From highly publicized recent history, they would have known that a jury had stood up to the court in New York and acquitted John Peter Zenger of "seditious libel" for publishing true but critical stories about the colonial governor, despite being admonished by the judge that "truth is no defense." And they were well aware that colonial juries had refused to apply the Navigation Acts to sea captains who had brought goods to the colonies without first pay-ing Mother England for the privilege of doing so: they had just recently won a war of independence, declared in part because England had been extraditing these sea captains and trying them without juries.

Jury nullification in the 1800s

What Jefferson and his like-minded colleagues did not know was that their concept of the jury would be perverted a little over a century later by the U.S. Supreme Court. Their writings used the word "jury" as it was defined at the time, as in Noah Webster's original dictionary, which he published in 1828 in order to preserve the integrity of the language of the U.S. Constitution: "Petty juries, consisting usually of twelve men, attend courts . . . to decide both the law and the fact in criminal prosecutions."

That definition, and jury instructions based upon it, were prevalent during the 18th and 19th centuries, and lingered to some degree even after *Sparf and Hansen*. Both the intent and the result of juries judging "both law and fact" was exactly as intended by the Founders. It gave the citizens a routine and effective handle on the government: they could say "no" to the prosecution of an accused person if they disapproved of the law itself or the way it was being used. Not only did this do much to ensure that justice was served, it sent powerful messages back to the lawmakers—to rework or repeal legislation that the people were refusing to apply.

In other words, in addition to providing a way for the accused to receive justice at the hands of his peers in the courtroom, the Founders expected the institution of trial by jury to "check and balance" the entire government. They did not expect such performance out of democratic elections, recall procedures, constitutional referenda, free speech, law making, or any other institution, political or otherwise. When Jefferson said that trial by jury was the "only anchor," he meant exactly that.

Nonetheless, periodic objections from the courts of the land were heard on occasion, as early as the 1820s and 1830s. One argument was that because bad law was no longer sent here from England, American jurors would no longer "need" the power to reject it. And besides, Americans could now "have their say on the law" through their elected representatives.

> *Without the . . . check and balance power which juries were intended to exert, our constitutional republic is rapidly degenerating into a police state.*

But the practice of informing the jury of its full range of powers remained widespread, and for decades functioned exactly as intended by the Founders. For example, in northern states, juries began awarding abused slaves with freedom as well as damages against their masters. The trend had resulted in legislatures outlawing slavery in most of the North by the time fugitive slave laws were passed, and it became difficult to find a jury which would convict either runaway slaves or underground railroaders charged under those laws. And juries had already begun awarding damages to slaves in southern states by the time the Civil War began. It was during this era that the courts began interrogating potential jurors to determine whether they agreed with the law—as a condition of serving! But a lot of people must have had their fingers crossed while they responded.

Juries also came to the rescue of organized labor in the late 1800s, when laws prohibiting striking were passed. Factory workers, faced with no other tool by which to defend the value or other conditions of their labor, struck anyway. Local juries proved very prone to relate to the plight of strikers and to acquit them, despite clear evidence that they had, indeed, stopped working and talked their fellow workers into doing likewise. Some historians cite pressure on the courts from Big Business to "do something" about these "runaway juries" as the hidden agenda behind the Supreme Court's decision in *Sparf and Hansen*.

A threat to citizens

In any event, since that time, few people have been apprised of their power as jurors. It's not taught in public (government) schools. Nor is it taught in college sociology or political science classes. And most law schools don't cover the subject of jury nullification, either. Worst of all, it's not explained in the courtrooms of the land to the people who most need to know about it—the jurors. Judges only rarely so inform the jury, and lawyers can face contempt charges if they insist on "telling" the jury without prior approval from the bench.

The results have been disastrous. Not only are our jails packed with harmless people, but special-interest laws of every description (inevitably disguised as laws designed to serve the common good) have multiplied into the millions, unchecked by jury review. The worst of these laws have created "crimes against the state," otherwise known as "political crimes" or "victimless crimes." These were unknown under the common law, and unenforceable in the heyday of fully informed, fully empowered trial juries.

In short, without the bottom-line check and balance power which juries were intended to exert, our constitutional republic is rapidly degenerating into a police state. To the extent that interest groups can get laws passed to suit themselves, and the largest and most powerful interest group is a government which can regularly hoodwink the citizen juries into enforcing these laws against fellow citizens, America faces imminent totalitarian control.

Clearly, the road back to constitutional government is to restore the power of the jury. It's been over sixty years since jury veto power struck its last major blow for freedom, when uncounted thousands of acquittals by jury made Prohibition politically unsustainable, and it was repealed. Like the fugitive slave laws, it was a case of special-interest law discarded by a rights-conscious citizenry.

The 19th century also produced scholars who had much appreciation for the power of the jury, such as Lysander Spooner. In his 1852 book *Trial by Jury*, Spooner stressed the political importance of jury veto power to the continued health of the Republic. Though he never had to take to the streets for jury veto power because the problems he anticipated were years away, fulfillment of Spooner's predictions underlies much of today's movement for a return to "Fully Informed Juries."

For example, he correctly predicted that juries would be reduced to "finders of fact," while the government would decide both the law and how the jury should apply it. And he warned that the government could therefore make absolutely anything illegal, and would do so in its inevitable quest to enslave the citizenry, unless stopped in its tracks by jury nullification.

The Fully Informed Jury Association

It's far too late now to prevent the damage that Spooner foresaw, but a grassroots organization known as the Fully Informed Jury Association (FIJA) believes that if there's a chink in the armor of the juggernaut, it's in telling the juries of America that they can vote on the verdict according to conscience. FIJA's goal is to reverse damage already done, and to prevent its recurrence.

According to founders of the organization Larry Dodge and Don Doig, "it all began" when Larry took in a lecture by M.J. "Red" Beckman, Montana's "Fighting Redhead" tax resister. Red challenged his audience by saying he was going to tell them something about their Constitution that they didn't already know. It was actually quite a challenge, since it was delivered to delegates at a 1979 Montana Libertarian Party convention. But Red made good. He explained the power of the jury and its constitutional basis, and no one in the audience could say he or she "knew that already."

But it wasn't until eight years later that a second exposure to the idea caused Larry to see just how *generally* jury veto power could apply to the laws of the land, especially to victimless or "political" crime laws, his nemesis. At an "initiatives fair" which Larry organized as the main event for the 1987 Montana Libertarian Party convention, one of the citizen initiatives proposed would have required the courts of Montana to inform all trial jurors of their veto power.

To be against the idea of telling juries about their power is to espouse misinforming them that they must follow the law, like it or not.

That was the spark which inspired Larry to consult with longtime fellow freedom fighter Don Doig, and "get something going." The idea seemed to have few, if any holes in it: (1) procedure in both state and federal courts is subject to statute law; (2) legal bases for jury nullification already exist in both constitutional and case law (even in *Sparf and Hansen*, the majority opinion acknowledges—but rues—the power of the jury to disregard the law, yet says that the Court would respect any state law or tradition which requires that jurors shall be so told); (3) jury veto power is relatively easily explained—and once explained, the job is done; (4) it has the potential to become a very broad-based movement, because the proliferation of crimes against the state has adversely affected practically everyone by now, giving people from every walk of life at least some personal incentive to work for restoration of jury power; and (5) it's within the realm of the possible, because it only requires reminding people of a power they already have, instead of asking that they chart a new course for the American Dream.

All of the above assumptions proved to be true, at least to some extent. Resistance on the part of legislatures to enact "FIJA" laws was stiff at first, but now that various state FIJA organizations have grown stronger, and have been lobbying for several years, proposed FIJA legislation is gaining ground, passing one house in each of two states in 1993, with several possible success stories in sight for 1995.

That's in part because many legislators are now satisfied, after doing some homework, that fully informed juries are indeed part of our judicial heritage after all. Liking that idea has come instantly for some lawmakers, but glacially or not at all for others. Most of the opposition has come from those whose vested interests lie in maintaining the (political) crime wave, such as law enforcement and district attorney associations, or people who build or operate prisons, and some judges.

But for lawmakers and interest groups alike, the truth about jury veto power is translating into receptivity. At this point, to deny its reality is to express one's ignorance. To be against the idea of telling juries about their power is to espouse misinforming them that they must follow the law, like it or not. It's to say the justice system (not to mention the rest of our government) works best when citizens are deliberately kept ignorant of their rights and powers, especially when called upon to judge their fellows.

9

Jury Nullification Should Not Be Allowed

Mark S. Pulliam

Mark S. Pulliam is an attorney in San Diego, California.

Jury nullification occurs when juries that disagree with the law or the law's application acquit guilty defendants. Supporters of jury nullification believe it is acceptable as a form of civil disobedience against unjust laws or as a kind of popular opposition to unreasonable government authority. However, the jury is not an appropriate place for activist resistance. Jurors take an oath before a trial to consider only the presented evidence and the judge's instructions. For justice to be served, jurors must apply the law despite any moral or political objections they might have.

What do nineteenth-century anarchist Lysander Spooner,[1] the O.J. Simpson legal defense team, some elements of the militia movement,[2] the Los Angeles juries that failed to convict the Menendez brothers of murdering their parents and that acquitted the brutal assailants of Reginald Denny, and the activists who promote the idea of "fully informed juries"[3] have in common?

They all symbolize the notion that juries can and should refuse to heed the instructions given them by the trial judge, and that jurors should instead follow their own consciences and "nullify" those instructions by doing what they personally feel is just.

Jury instructions are the applicable legal rules communicated to the jury by the trial judge. In virtually every jurisdiction, jurors take an oath at the beginning of the case that they will consider only the evidence presented and the instructions of the court. The "instructions" are, therefore, laws that society has duly enacted through either the legislative process or the common law judicial process. In either event, the laws derive legitimacy from our democratic political traditions.

As citizens, we may not agree with all the laws on the books, but in a system of representative government we are bound to follow them. It is inherent in the concept of the State that there will not be unanimity in

Mark S. Pulliam, "Nullifying the Rule of Law," *Freeman*, March 1996. Copyright ©1996 by The Foundation for Economic Education. Reprinted with permission.

all matters, but that the views of the majority will prevail. This "coercion" or "oppression" of the dissenting minority has long perturbed anarchist philosophers such as the aforementioned Spooner, who objected to the "social compact" rationale for the state as well as the institution of the jury.[4] Jury-power activists sometimes cite Spooner as a proponent of "jury nullification," but he is best known for his more fundamental objection to constitutional government.

On what basis do advocates of jury nullification attempt to justify the lawlessness that ignoring the court's instructions entails? Advocates advance two principal explanations, neither of which is persuasive: (1) civil disobedience, or the moral right or obligation to resist enforcement of an unjust law,[5] and (2) populist opposition to tyrannical actions by an unresponsive government.[6] Let's consider these explanations.

Civil disobedience

Civil disobedience is a misnomer in the context of a seated juror refusing to follow the law. Civil disobedience, properly understood, is resistance to unjust government action as a last resort—when disobedience is the only alternative to becoming a participant in an objectionable act. This will never be the case with a seated juror. A potential juror who objected to service could refuse to report to court or serve on a jury. A person with a moral objection to enforcing a particular law (say, punishing a defendant charged with private drug use or blockading abortion clinics) could disclose that objection during voir dire [jury selection] and be excused from serving in the case.

But, after a juror has reported for service, been screened through voir dire, been seated and sworn to follow the law according to the instructions of the court, there is no room for "civil disobedience." A juror reneging on his oath is an outlaw, a scofflaw. A renegade juror cheats the parties to the case out of their right to have the matter decided according to the law, on the basis of which the evidence and arguments have been presented.

Despite proponents' fondness of quoting Henry David Thoreau on civil disobedience,[7] a lawless juror is no more heroic than a rogue policeman violating the law or a politician accepting a bribe. If a juror (or any other member of the political community) feels that a particular law is unjust—and in a society as large and diverse as ours, we can assume that someone, somewhere, feels that every law on the books is unjust—the remedy is to petition the legislature for reform, not to infiltrate the jury and then ignore the law.

Populist opposition

The other frequently cited justification for jury nullification—the need to rein in abusive government power—is even more specious. An honest anarchist such as Lysander Spooner would refuse to serve on a jury because he wouldn't believe in the concept of mandatory jury service or even governmental proceedings to enforce the law. Let's not forget that a trial, whether civil or criminal, *is* government action. Enforcing democratically enacted laws is one of the basic purposes of government. When a juror considers defying his oath and deciding a case based on his personal feelings rather than the court's instructions, the alternative is not between liberty and coercion, but between coercion informed by the rule of law and coercion at the whim of 12 jurors.

And what is a jury acting outside of the law but a 12-person mob, like modern-day vigilantes? Although the jury-power activists point to historical events where juries refused to enforce the Fugitive Slave Act,[8] there is no assurance that a jury operating outside the law would only acquit in a criminal case; it could just as easily "nullify" the instructions by convicting a person who was technically innocent. Moreover, there are no counterparts to the Fugitive Slave Law in a civil case. Furthermore, nullifying the law strips the individuals who comprise society of *their* right to have the laws enforced. Nothing could be more tyrannical or despotic than the arbitrary decision of a jury that has rejected the law.

A lawless juror is no more heroic than a rogue policeman violating the law or a politician accepting a bribe.

It disturbs me to see libertarians and conservatives—whom I generally regard as allies—embrace the jury nullification cause. The rule of law is essential to the preservation of liberty. Friedrich Hayek, perhaps the twentieth century's pre-eminent theorist of classical liberalism—the political philosophy of freedom—believed that the defining characteristic of a free society is the rule of law, meaning legal rules stated in advance, uniformly applied, without excessive discretion.[9] In Hayek's words: "[W]hen we obey laws, in the sense of general abstract rules laid down irrespective of their application to us, we are not subject to another man's will and are therefore free."[10] Thus, it is the universal, non-selective nature of law that allows us to be free.[11] In Hayek's view, it is precisely because judges and juries cannot pick and choose what laws to enforce in a particular case "that it can be said that laws and not men rule."[12] Jury-activist pamphleteers in front of the courthouse would do well to heed Hayek's admonition that "few beliefs have been more destructive of the respect for the rules of law and of morals than the idea that a rule is binding only if the beneficial effect of observing it in the particular instance can be recognized."[13]

Yet that is exactly what advocates of jury nullification espouse—following the law only if they agree with it in a particular case. I am not unsympathetic to concerns about unjust laws and government overreaching. The solution is grassroots political activism and reforms such as fewer federal mandates and expanded use of the initiative and recall devices, not shortsighted demagoguery in the form of jury nullification. Jurors ignoring the law accomplish nothing but anarchy in a microcosm—nullifying the rule of law.

Notes

1. Lysander Spooner, *An Essay on the Trial By Jury* (1852).

2. "Militias Are Joining Jury-Power Activists to Fight Government," *Wall Street Journal* (May 25, 1995), p. A1 (hereinafter "Militias").

3. *Ibid.*

4. Lysander Spooner, *No Treason: The Constitution of No Authority* (1870).

5. Michael Pierone, "Requiring Citizens to Do Evil," *The Freeman* (July 1993), p. 261.

6. "Militias," p. A8; N. Stephan Kinsella, "Legislation and Law in a Free Society," *The Freeman* (September 1995), pp. 561, 563.

7. Pierone, note 5, p. 262.

8. *Ibid.*

9. Friedrich A. Hayek, *The Road to Serfdom* (Chicago: University of Chicago Press, 1944), pp. 72–79.

10. Friedrich A. Hayek, *The Constitution of Liberty* (Chicago: University of Chicago Press, 1960), p. 153.

11. *Ibid.*, pp. 153–54.

12. *Ibid.*, p. 153.

13. *Ibid.*, p. 159.

10

Selected Racially Based Nullification Can Create Justice

Paul Butler

Paul Butler is an associate professor of law at the George Washington University Law School.

Jury nullification—the acquittal of guilty defendants by jurors expressing disagreement with the law—should be exercised by black jurors who are chosen for trials involving nonviolent black defendants. Presently, one-third of young African American men are incarcerated, awaiting trial, on probation, or on parole. The absence of these young men has damaged the black community both socially and economically. Furthermore, the criminal-justice system, which is controlled by mostly white lawmakers, often discriminates against black defendants and does not reflect African American concepts of justice. For these reasons, black jurors have a moral mandate to vote for the acquittal of nonviolent black lawbreakers.

In 1990 I was a Special Assistant United States Attorney in the District of Columbia. I prosecuted people accused of misdemeanor crimes, mainly the drug and gun cases that overwhelm the local courts of most American cities. As a federal prosecutor, I represented the United States of America and used that power to put people, mainly African-American men, in prison. I am also an African-American man. During that time, I made two discoveries that profoundly changed the way I viewed my work as a prosecutor and my responsibilities as a black person.

The first discovery occurred during a training session for new assistants conducted by experienced prosecutors. We rookies were informed that we would lose many of our cases, despite having persuaded a jury beyond a reasonable doubt that the defendant was guilty. We would lose because some black jurors would refuse to convict black defendants who they knew were guilty.

The second discovery was related to the first but was even more un-

Paul Butler, "Black Jurors: Right to Acquit?" *Harper's Magazine*, December 1995; adapted from "Racially Based Jury Nullification: Black Power in the Criminal Justice System," *Yale Law Journal*, December 1995. Reprinted by permission of the Yale Law Journal Company and Fred B. Rothman & Company.

settling. It occurred during the trial of Marion Barry, then the second-term mayor of the District of Columbia. Barry was being prosecuted by my office for drug possession and perjury. I learned, to my surprise, that some of my fellow African-American prosecutors hoped that the mayor would be acquitted, despite the fact that he was obviously guilty of at least one of the charges—an FBI videotape plainly showed him smoking crack cocaine. These black prosecutors wanted their office to lose its case because they believed that the prosecution of Barry was racist.

There is an increasing perception that some African-American jurors vote to acquit black defendants for racial reasons, sometimes explained as the juror's desire not to send another black man to jail. There is considerable disagreement over whether it is appropriate for a black juror to do so. I now believe that, for pragmatic and political reasons, the black community is better off when some non-violent lawbreakers remain in the community rather than go to prison. The decision as to what kind of conduct by African Americans ought to be punished is better made by African Americans, based on their understanding of the costs and benefits to their community, than by the traditional criminal justice process, which is controlled by white lawmakers and white law enforcers. Legally, African-American jurors who sit in judgment of African-American accused persons have the power to make that decision. Considering the costs of law enforcement to the black community, and the failure of white lawmakers to come up with any solutions to black antisocial conduct other than incarceration, it is, in fact, the moral responsibility of black jurors to emancipate some guilty black outlaws.

Distrusting the system

Why would a black juror vote to let a guilty person go free? Assuming the juror is a rational, self-interested actor, she must believe that she is better off with the defendant out of prison than in prison. But how could any rational person believe that about a criminal?

Imagine a country in which a third of the young male citizens are under the supervision of the criminal justice system—either awaiting trial, in prison, or on probation or parole. Imagine a country in which two-thirds of the men can anticipate being arrested before they reach age thirty. Imagine a country in which there are more young men in prison than in college.

The country imagined above is a police state. When we think of a police state, we think of a society whose fundamental problem lies not with the citizens of the state but rather with the form of government, and with the powerful elites in whose interest the state exists. Similarly, racial critics of American criminal justice locate the problem not with the black prisoners but with the state and its actors and beneficiaries.

The black community also bears very real costs by having so many African Americans, particularly males, incarcerated or otherwise involved in the criminal justice system. These costs are both social and economic, and they include the large percentage of black children who live in female-headed, single-parent households; a perceived dearth of men "eligible" for marriage; the lack of male role models for black children, especially boys; the absence of wealth in the black community; and the large unemployment rate among black men.

According to a *USA Today*/CNN/Gallup poll, 66 percent of blacks believe that the criminal justice system is racist and only 32 percent believe it is not racist. Interestingly, other polls suggest that blacks also tend to be more worried about crime than whites; this seems logical when one considers that blacks are more likely to be victims of crime. This enhanced concern, however, does not appear to translate to black support for tougher enforcement of criminal law. For example, substantially fewer blacks than whites support the death penalty, and many more blacks than whites were concerned with the potential racial consequences of the strict provisions of 1994's crime bill. Along with significant evidence from popular culture, these polls suggest that a substantial portion of the African-American community sympathizes with racial critiques of the criminal justice system.

The power to acquit

African-American jurors who endorse these critiques are in a unique position to act on their beliefs when they sit in judgment of a black defendant. As jurors, they have the power to convict the accused person or to set him free. May the responsible exercise of that power include voting to free a black defendant who the juror believes is guilty? The answer is "yes," based on the legal doctrine known as jury nullification.

Jury nullification occurs when a jury acquits a defendant who it believes is guilty of the crime with which he is charged. In finding the defendant not guilty, the jury ignores the facts of the case and/or the judge's instructions regarding the law. Instead, the jury votes its conscience.

The prerogative of juries to nullify has been part of English and American law for centuries. There are well-known cases from the Revolutionary War era when American patriots were charged with political crimes by the British crown and acquitted by American juries. Black slaves who escaped to the North and were prosecuted for violation of the Fugitive Slave Law were freed by Northern juries with abolitionist sentiments. Some Southern juries refused to punish white violence against African Americans, especially black men accused of crimes against white women.

The Supreme Court has officially disapproved of jury nullification but has conceded that it has no power to prohibit jurors from engaging in it; the Bill of Rights does not allow verdicts of acquittal to be reversed, regardless of the reason for the acquittal. Criticism of nullification has centered on its potential for abuse. The criticism suggests that when twelve members of a jury vote their conscience instead of the law, they corrupt the rule of law and undermine the democratic principles that made the law.

There is no question that jury nullification is subversive of the rule of law. Nonetheless, most legal historians agree that it was morally appropriate in the cases of the white American revolutionaries and the runaway slaves. The issue, then, is whether African Americans today have the moral right to engage in this same subversion.

Most moral justifications of the obligation to obey the law are based on theories of "fair play." Citizens benefit from the rule of law; that is why it is just that they are burdened with the requirement to follow it. Yet most blacks are aware of countless historical examples in which

African Americans were not afforded the benefit of the rule of law: think, for example, of the existence of slavery in a republic purportedly dedicated to the proposition that all men are created equal, or the law's support of state-sponsored segregation even after the Fourteenth Amendment guaranteed blacks equal protection. That the rule of law ultimately corrected some of the large holes in the American fabric is evidence more of its malleability than its goodness; the rule of law previously had justified the holes.

If the rule of law is a myth, or at least not valid for African Americans, the argument that jury nullification undermines it loses force. The black juror is simply another actor in the system, using her power to fashion a particular outcome. The juror's act of nullification—like the act of the citizen who dials 911 to report Ricky but not Bob, or the police officer who arrests Lisa but not Mary, or the prosecutor who charges Kwame but not Brad, or the judge who finds that Nancy was illegally entrapped but Verna was not—exposes the indeterminacy of law but does not in itself create it.

A similar argument can be made regarding the criticism that jury nullification is anti-democratic. This is precisely why many African Americans endorse it; it is perhaps the only legal power black people have to escape the tyranny of the majority. Black people have had to beg white decision makers for most of the rights they have: the right not to be slaves, the right to vote, the right to attend an integrated school. Now black people are begging white people to preserve programs that help black children to eat and black businesses to survive. Jury nullification affords African Americans the power to determine justice for themselves, in individual cases, regardless of whether white people agree or even understand.

Ethical nullification

At this point, African Americans should ask themselves whether the operation of the criminal law system in the United States advances the interests of black people. If it does not, the doctrine of jury nullification affords African-American jurors the opportunity to exercise the authority of the law over some African-American criminal defendants. In essence, black people can "opt out" of American criminal law.

How far should they go—completely to anarchy, or is there someplace between here and there that is safer than both? I propose the following: African-American jurors should approach their work cognizant of its political nature and of their prerogative to exercise their power in the best interests of the black community. In every case, the juror should be guided by her view of what is "just." (I have more faith, I should add, in the average black juror's idea of justice than I do in the idea that is embodied in the "rule of law.")

In cases involving violent *malum in se* (inherently bad) crimes, such as murder, rape, and assault, jurors should consider the case strictly on the evidence presented, and if they believe the accused person is guilty, they should so vote. In cases involving non-violent, *malum prohibitum* (legally proscribed) offenses, including "victimless" crimes such as narcotics possession, there should be a presumption in favor of nullification. Finally, for non-violent, *malum in se* crimes, such as theft or perjury, there need be no presumption in favor of nullification, but it ought to be an option the juror considers. A juror might vote for acquittal, for example, when a poor woman steals from Tiffany's but not when the same woman steals from her next-door neighbor.

How would a juror decide individual cases under my proposal? Easy cases would include a defendant who has possessed crack cocaine and an abusive husband who kills his wife. The former should be acquitted and the latter should go to prison.

The black community is better off when some non-violent lawbreakers remain in the community rather than go to prison.

Difficult scenarios would include the drug dealer who operates in the ghetto and the thief who burglarizes the home of a rich white family. Under my proposal, nullification is presumed in the first case because drug distribution is a non-violent *malum prohibitum* offense. Is nullification morally justifiable here? It depends. There is no question that encouraging people to engage in self-destructive behavior is evil; the question the juror should ask herself is whether the remedy is less evil. (The juror should also remember that the criminal law does not punish those ghetto drug dealers who cause the most injury: liquor store owners.)

As for the burglar who steals from the rich white family, the case is troubling, first of all, because the conduct is so clearly "wrong." Since it is a non-violent *malum in se* crime, there is no presumption in favor of nullification, but it is an option for consideration. Here again, the facts of the case are relevant. For example, if the offense was committed to support a drug habit, I think there is a moral case to be made for nullification, at least until such time as access to drug-rehabilitation services are available to all.

Why would a juror be inclined to follow my proposal? There is no guarantee that she would. But when we perceive that black jurors are already nullifying on the basis of racial critiques (i.e., refusing to send another black man to jail), we recognize that these jurors are willing to use their power in a politically conscious manner. Further, it appears that some black jurors now excuse some conduct—like murder—that they should not excuse. My proposal provides a principled structure for the exercise of the black juror's vote. I am not encouraging anarchy; rather I am reminding black jurors of their privilege to serve a calling higher than law: justice.

I concede that the justice my proposal achieves is rough. It is as susceptible to human foibles as the jury system. But I am sufficiently optimistic that my proposal will be only an intermediate plan, a stopping point between the status quo and real justice. To get to that better, middle ground, I hope that this essay will encourage African Americans to use responsibly the power they already have.

11

Racially Based Jury Nullification Is Not Just

Michael Weiss and Karl Zinsmeister

Michael Weiss is an attorney in Houston, Texas, and a senior fellow at the Texas Public Policy Foundation in Galveston. Karl Zinsmeister is a DeWitt Wallace Fellow of the American Enterprise Institute and the editor of the American Enterprise, *a bimonthly conservative journal.*

Race-based jury nullification occurs when jurors (usually black jurors) assert their disagreement with the law by refusing to convict members of their own race. Supporters of race-based jury nullification believe that racism is endemic in society's institutions, creating an environment that breeds criminal behavior. Because institutionalized racism is largely responsible for crimes committed by racial minorities, they argue, minority defendants should be acquitted. In actuality, however, race-based jury nullification is discriminatory because it favors minority offenders over white offenders. In a criminal-justice system that strives to be fair, minority lawbreakers should receive the same treatment as whites who commit the same crimes.

In 1992, a white congressional aide working for Senator Richard Shelby of Alabama was shot to death in his Capitol Hill home. A few weeks later, a young black man named Edward Evans was arrested for the crime. Two of his friends testified that they saw him shoot the young aide; one said that Evans harbored strong anti-white sentiments and had earlier vowed to kill a white man. Although this and the material evidence presented what seemed to be an overwhelming case against Evans, one African American juror refused to convict. A frustrated jury foreman told the judge that Velma McNeil would simply not give any credence to the prosecution's evidence. A hung jury and mistrial resulted. A *Washington Post* photograph showed McNeil emerging from the courtroom hugging a relative of the accused murderer.

• In 1994, a Towson State college student who became lost in the Dutch Village section of Baltimore was robbed and murdered by Davon

Karl Zinsmeister and Michael Weiss, "When Race Trumps Truth in Court," *American Enterprise*, January/February 1996. Reprinted by permission of the *American Enterprise*, a Washington, D.C.-based magazine of business, politics, and culture.

Neverdon. After the student willingly handed over his wallet, Neverdon shot him in the face. Prosecutors presented four eyewitnesses who testified they saw Neverdon kill the man. Two other witnesses reported that Neverdon told them afterwards that he committed the murder. The evidence against Neverdon was so strong he bargained for a forty year sentence in exchange for a guilty plea, an offer which was rejected by the prosecution at the request of the victim's family. Yet a jury comprised of eleven African Americans and one Pakistani acquitted Neverdon because of "witness credibility" problems. Before the verdict, the Pakistani juror reported that "race may be playing some part" in the jury's decision.

• In another Baltimore case, a white man was killed when a cinder block was dropped on his head from a third floor balcony of a public housing project. Three witnesses identified the black defendant as the murderer and another testified in court that the defendant had confessed to him. The defendant was acquitted.

• After off-duty black police officer Rudy Thomas was murdered in Brooklyn in 1994, defendant Johnny Williams confessed to the crime on videotape, describing his motive and the murder weapon. Williams's fingerprints were found on the slain officer's motorcycle, and bullets from his gun matched those found in the victim. There were also three eyewitnesses to the crime. "We had enough evidence to supply three or four cases," reports the prosecuting attorney. But the defense claimed, with no evidence, that Williams was beaten by the white detective on the case, and a hung jury resulted. A juror who refused to give in to those favoring acquittal reported the deliberations were "blatantly racial."

• In 1994, a suburban white woman named Rebecca Gordon was driving through Detroit when she was gunned down by a group of blacks in an adjoining car. Defense counsel played the "race card" at the 1995 trial, and the inner city jury refused to convict defendant Brian Marable of murder, turning in a guilty verdict only on the misdemeanor charge of reckless discharge of a firearm.

At least one-fourth of all criminal cases that end in acquittal may involve some form of racial nullification.

• Darryl Smith, a black drug dealer in Washington, D.C., tortured eighteen-year-old African American Willie Wilson to death as he begged for mercy in front of witnesses. Despite massive amounts of evidence linking him to the crime, an all-black D.C. jury acquitted Smith in his 1990 murder trial. According to other jurors, forewoman Valerie Blackmon refused to convict because "she didn't want to send any more young black men to jail." After long deliberations, other members of the panel caved in to Blackmon's argument that the "criminal justice system is stacked against blacks" and let Smith off, though most believed that he was guilty. Three weeks after the verdict, a letter from an anonymous juror arrived at D.C. Superior Court expressing regret over the verdict.

• On August 19, 1991, after a traffic accident in which a black child was killed by a car carrying a Jewish leader, a black mob rioted down a street in the Crown Heights section of Brooklyn, shouting "Let's go get the Jews." A Jewish scholar visiting New York named Yankel Rosenbaum was stabbed to death when they encountered him on the street. Within minutes police arrived and apprehended Lemrick Nelson, Jr. at the scene with a bloody knife in his pocket. He was taken to the dying Rosenbaum, who identified Nelson as his attacker. Nelson later admitted the crime to two Brooklyn detectives, and signed a written confession. Prosecutors presented this evidence to a predominantly black jury. They refused to convict Nelson. After the acquittal, jurors celebrated with Nelson at a local restaurant. (Nelson later moved to Georgia and was convicted of slashing a schoolmate.)

Racialized legal bias

Clearly, there has been a booming trade in black racism in American courtrooms for some time. Then came the O.J. Simpson verdict. "The jury did not deliberate, it emoted," observed commentator Mona Charen afterwards. "If the prosecution's case was so weak, why did Johnnie Cochran argue in his summation that jurors disregard the evidence? . . . The reaction of so many American blacks to the verdict was unseemly and offensive. . . . One of the jurors, a former member of the Black Panther party, gave the black power salute" to Simpson in court right after the acquittal. "Was the jury fair-minded? Is black America?" asks Charen. "Only a nation of fools would lull itself into believing that this was not a racially motivated and a racist verdict." She warns that even "if Marcia Clark had produced a videotape of the murders in progress, the defense would have argued that the filmmaker was a racist and the jury would have found 'reasonable doubt.'"

Charen's videotape scenario is actually not so far-fetched. Racial legal bias exists not only at the street level among black Americans but also high among today's black leadership. This was clearly illustrated by an article published in December 1995 in the *Yale Law Journal*, and excerpted in the December 1995 *Harper's Magazine*. In it, a black George Washington University law professor and former prosecutor in the U.S. Attorney's office in the District of Columbia named Paul Butler describes how "during the trial of Marion Barry, then the second-term mayor of the District of Columbia, Barry was being prosecuted by my office for drug possession and perjury. I learned, to my surprise, that some of my fellow African American prosecutors hoped that the mayor would be acquitted, despite the fact that he was obviously guilty of at least one of the charges—an FBI videotape plainly showed him smoking crack cocaine. These black prosecutors wanted their office to lose its case because they believed that the prosecution of Barry was racist."

In his *Yale Law Journal* and *Harper's Magazine* articles, Butler makes it clear that racialized justice is not only a thriving inner city practice, but also a theory built on determined black intellectual rationalizations. He himself is a case in point. "During a training session for new assistants conducted by experienced prosecutors," he recalls, "we rookies were informed that we would lose many of our cases, despite having persuaded a jury beyond a reasonable doubt that the defendant was guilty. We would lose because some black jurors would refuse to convict black defendants who they knew were guilty . . . some African American jurors vote to acquit black defendants for racial reasons." Though he was then serving as a prosecutor of drug and gun criminals, Butler himself was soon converted to "the juror's desire not to send another black man to jail." Describing America as "a police state," he currently argues that for "pragmatic and political reasons," black jurors have a "moral responsibility . . . to emancipate some guilty black outlaws."

Noting that polls show 66 percent of blacks believe the U.S. criminal justice system is racist, Butler points out that "African American jurors who endorse these critiques are in a unique position to act on their beliefs when they sit in judgment of a black defendant." Today's African Americans "should ask themselves whether the operation of the criminal law system in the United States advances the interests of black people," and if they believe it does not, he urges, they should "opt out," judging defendants by whatever standards they please rather than by the law. This is known as jury nullification.

Butler presents some specific suggestions as to how black juries might take the law into their own hands. He urges that for crimes like drug dealing, gun possession, theft, and perjury, nullification always ought to be considered. He calls for African Americans to exercise double standards as they see fit: "A juror might vote for acquittal, for example, when a poor woman steals from Tiffany's but not when the same woman steals from her next-door neighbor." Specifically conjuring up a case of a black "thief who burglarizes the home of a rich white family," Butler sees "a moral case to be made for nullification."

Black jurors distrust prosecutors

Certainly big city prosecutors will tell you that they see lots of racialized jury-behavior. Lead prosecutor Marcia Clark told CNN after the Simpson acquittal that "a majority black jury won't bring a conviction in a case like this." She later scurried to retract that "off the record" statement, but other officials are not so shy. Los Angeles County deputy district attorney Bobby Grace states that "growing resentment . . . can affect a jury verdict." Atlanta-area assistant district attorney Leigh Dupre estimates that at least one-fourth of all criminal cases that end in acquittal may involve some form of racial nullification.

Prosecutors agree that urban black jurors have turned extremely skeptical of prosecution witnesses, especially police officers. Brooklyn district attorney Charles Hynes states that "the problem my office faced in court in the Yankel Rosenbaum trial is one that confronts prosecutors in most urban areas today: distrust by inner-city residents of the police officers who are sworn to protect and serve them." Bob Agacinski, deputy chief of the Wayne County prosecutors in Detroit, blames defense counsel for introducing this "racial appeal to juries . . . especially in cases where the witnesses are police officers. Police credibility is easy to attack . . . and juries are buying the argument that the police are looking to lock up any black man. . . . Minor inconsistencies in police testimony become reasonable doubt when the case has racial overtones." Racial pleas are "notoriously overused" by defense counsel, says Agacinski. He estimates that over "50 percent of the cases which go to trial involve some type of racial appeal."

Prosecutors have noted a "more blatant use" of the racial defense since the Simpson trial began. In the summer of 1994, for instance, after an elderly man was beaten to death by a black defendant at a Detroit-area McDonald's, defense attorneys invoked racial sympathies even though the defendant confessed the murder to police officers. They claimed the confession was coerced by the white officers, and the predominantly black jury voted to acquit.

Racial pleas are "notoriously overused" by defense counsel.

Rogue cops really do exist, as the vile Mark Fuhrman reminded us. But at present, *every* cop is viewed as a rogue by many inner-city jurors. "Police officers now have to prove that race was *not* an issue in an arrest," reports a former prosecutor in the U.S. attorney's office in Washington, D.C. Baltimore assistant state attorney Ahmet Hisim illustrates the problem using a rating scale. In a typical city today, he says, "black jurors will automatically assess at least thirty points out of a hundred against a police officer's credibility, without even hearing any testimony."

Defense counsel are also quick to attack the credibility of non-police prosecution witnesses. A former assistant U.S. attorney in D.C. maintains that "in major metropolitan cities where prosecutors deal with predominantly black juries, defense counsel will put the government on trial because of the kinds of witnesses that the government must use." Often the prosecution has to rely on informants involved in the same kinds of activity as the defendant, and today's suspicious juries leap to discount their testimony. Determined skepticism of this sort can be very difficult to overcome. D.C. Detective Donald Gossage, who worked on the Darryl Smith case, notes that "you don't have your nuns and doctors and lawyers standing on these street corners."

The outcome of racialized "justice"

In addition to prosecutors' estimates like the startling ones above from Detroit's Agacinski and Atlanta's Dupre, there are other small and localized indicators of increased racialism in court. More hung juries are one obvious sign. The black teenager who murdered English tourist Gary Colley at a Florida rest stop, for instance, had to be tried three times before he was convicted because his first two trials ended in hung juries. This despite the fact that he and his three teenage accomplices had more than a hundred arrests amongst them at the time of the murder. In California, there are currently between 10,000 and 11,000 hung juries annually—up to 15 percent of all cases tried. That figure represents a lot of foregone justice, and also a huge public expense, given that the average trial costs taxpayers $10,000 a day, according to the California District Attorney's Association.

Hard nationwide figures on acquittals by race of defendant, victim, and jury are hard to come by. Data from the U.S. Bureau of Justice Statistics do show that in the 75 largest counties in the U.S., rates of felony prosecution and conviction are slightly lower for blacks than whites. In a few jurisdictions where clear statistics are available, the patterns are dramatic. Nationwide, the felony acquittal rate for defendants of all races is only 17 percent, but in the Bronx, where more than eight out of ten jurors are black or Hispanic, 48 percent of all black felony defendants are acquitted. In Washington, D.C., where more than 95 percent of defendants and 70 percent of jurors are black, 29 percent of all felony trials ended in acquittal in 1994. In Wayne County, which includes mostly black Detroit, 30 percent of felony defendants are acquitted.

On the day of the O.J. Simpson acquittal, a veteran New York law enforcement official estimated off-handedly to criminologist John DiIulio that "there's 100,000 O.J.s. We've reached the point where the system is rigged to let murderers, and not just rich ones, escape justice."

What are the ultimate effects of this racialized judgment in U.S. courtrooms? Obviously there is tremendous personal hurt in cases where justice is not done, and the number of such cases is rising. There is also more disrespect for the law, and a lot more crime and society-wide damage done by perpetrators who should be locked up instead of roaming the streets.

Former U.S. attorney Joseph DiGenova argues that advocates of jury nullification on racial grounds are "pushing anarchy." The refusal to convict by black juries is "rampant" and getting worse, he warns, and this is feeding the inner-city crime cycle. DiGenova also notes that "we fought like hell to get blacks into the system as cops and prosecutors and judges, and now these guys are being fiercely ostracized and pressured, and told in their own community that a black person shouldn't work in such a position. Well, who *is* supposed to respond to black criminals? Or are we just supposed to pretend there aren't any black criminals?"

The refusal to convict [black defendants] by black juries. . . is feeding the inner-city crime cycle.

John DiIulio adds that big city prosecutors today view cases where there is a white victim and a black defendant as "no win situations." Recognizing that it will be difficult to get a conviction, prosecutors pull their punches: avoiding the death penalty like the plague even where it is clearly merited (like the Simpson case), avoiding multiple counts and other moves that might give the appearance of piling on, largely letting defense attorneys pick the juries, and trying desperately to plea bargain everything to avoid going to a jury in the first place. The result, DiIulio says, is that "blacks are being substantially and systematically underprosecuted today, not only in cases of black-on-white crime, but also in cases of black-on-black."

Baltimore prosecutor Hisim advises that it is dangerous for jurors to attempt to "fix the system by being revolutionary." Recognizing that "black jurors seem to be striking back at society," Hisim suggests that they should be educated about the consequences of racially-based nullification, since 90 percent of crime is committed by people living in a juror's own community. The irony is that by letting clearly guilty individuals go, jurors are only "infecting their own neighborhoods with criminals."

Organizations to Contact

The editors have compiled the following list of organizations concerned with the issues debated in this book. The descriptions are derived from materials provided by the organizations themselves. All have publications or information available for interested readers. The list was compiled on the date of publication of the present volume; names, addresses, phone and fax numbers, and e-mail/internet addresses may change. Be aware that many organizations take several weeks or longer to respond to inquiries, so allow as much time as possible.

ABA Criminal Justice Standards Committee
Criminal Justice Section
740 15th St. NW
Washington, DC 20005
(202) 662-1500
fax: (202) 662-1501

The American Bar Association's Criminal Justice Section comprises attorneys, law students, judges, law professors, and law enforcement personnel interested in the quick, fair, and effective administration of criminal justice. The Criminal Justice Standards Committee is one of more than twenty committees that address the services and functions of defense attorneys and prosecutors. The committee publishes the book *ABA Standards for Criminal Justice: Discovery and Trial by Jury*.

Brookings Institution
1775 Massachusetts Ave. NW
Washington, DC 20036
(202) 797-6000
fax: (202) 797-6004

Founded in 1927, the Brookings Institution is a liberal research and educational organization that publishes material on economics, government, and foreign policy. The institution produces books and papers on the jury system and publishes analyses of the legal system in its quarterly magazine the *Brookings Review*.

Committee for Modern Courts
19 W. 44th St., Suite 1200
New York, NY 10036
(212) 575-1577
fax: (212) 869-1133

The committee is an organization concerned with the quality and administration of justice. It opposes any efforts to eliminate the right to trial by jury explicitly provided in the U.S. Constitution. The committee publishes the position paper "Goal: A Juror's Bill of Rights" and the quarterly newsletter *Modern Courts*.

Fully Informed Jury Association (FIJA)
PO Box 59
Helmville, MT 59843
(406) 793-5550
fax: (406) 793-5550

The association works to increase the effectiveness of the institution of trial by jury by the passage of the Fully Informed Jury Act (or Amendment). This act would require that criminal court judges instruct juries to judge both the law and the facts in reaching a verdict. The association publishes the *Jury Power Information Kit* and the quarterly newsletter *FIJActivist*.

National Center for State Courts (NCSC)
PO Box 8798
Williamsburg, VA 23187-8798
(804) 253-2000
fax: (804) 220-0449

The NCSC acts as a clearinghouse for information on improving the judicial system. It works to strengthen the structure and administration of trial and appellate courts, and it compiles statistics on state court caseloads and administrative operations. The center's publications include the book *Managing Notorious Cases* as well as the upcoming books *Jury System Management* and *Innovations in Jury Management*.

National Institute for Citizen Education in the Law (NICEL)
711 G St. SE
Washington, DC 20003
(202) 546-6644, ext. 228
fax: (202) 546-6649

The NICEL educates the public about issues concerning the legal system. It conducts student mock trials, teen action programs, and other law-related educational projects to promote knowledge and respect for the law. The institute publishes the semiannual *Street Law News* and various textbooks, articles, and brochures.

The Roscoe Pound Foundation
1050 31st St. NW
Washington, DC 20007
(202) 965-3500
fax: (202) 965-0355

A think tank for the Association of Trial Lawyers, the foundation works to strengthen the legal system by improving the trial bar and the jury system and by making the law more responsive to the needs of citizens. It publishes the book *The Jury in America* and also makes available the Association of Trial Lawyers brochure *The American Jury*.

Bibliography

Books

Jeffrey Abramson	*We, the Jury: The Jury System and the Ideal of Democracy.* New York: BasicBooks, 1994.
Stephen J. Adler	*The Jury: Trial and Error in the American Courtroom.* New York: Times Books, 1994.
American Bar Association	*ABA Standards for Criminal Justice: Discovery and Trial by Jury.* Chicago: American Bar Association, 1996.
Association of Trial Lawyers of America	*When Justice Is Up to You: Celebrating America's Guarantee of Trial by Jury.* Washington, DC: Association of Trial Lawyers of America, 1992.
Blanche Davis Blank	*The Not So Grand Jury: The Story of the Federal Grand Jury System.* Lanham, MD: University Press of America, 1993.
Stephen Daniels and Joanne Martin	*Civil Juries and the Politics of Reform.* Evanston, IL: Northwestern University Press, 1996.
Norbert Ehrenfreund and Lawrence Treat	*You're the Jury: Solve Twelve Real-Life Court Cases Along with the Juries Who Decided Them.* New York: Holt, 1992.
Norman J. Finkel	*Commonsense Justice: Jurors' Notions of the Law.* Cambridge, MA: Harvard University Press, 1995.
Hiroshi Fukurai, Edgar W. Butler, and Richard Krooth	*Race and the Jury: Racial Disenfranchisement and the Search for Justice.* New York: Plenum Press, 1993.
Michael Knox with Mike Walker	*The Private Diary of an O.J. Juror: Behind the Scenes of the Trial of the Century.* Beverly Hills, CA: Dove Books, 1994.
Robert E. Litan, ed.	*Verdict: Assessing the Civil Jury System.* Washington, DC: The Brookings Institution, 1993.
Hastie Reid, ed.	*Inside the Juror: The Psychology of Juror Decision-Making.* New York: Cambridge University Press, 1993.
Hazel Thornton	*Hung Jury: The Diary of a Menendez Juror.* Philadelphia: Temple University Press, 1994.
Neil Vidmar	*Medical Malpractice and the American Jury.* Ann Arbor: University of Michigan Press, 1996.

Periodicals

Stephen J. Adler	"Jury Trials and the Wizards of Odds," *American Enterprise*, November/December 1994.
Stewart Ain	"Aiming to Improve the Jury System," *New York Times*, February 12, 1995.

76

Albert W. Alshuler

"Our Faltering Jury," *Public Interest*, Winter 1996.

Akhil Reed Amar and
Vikram David Amar

"Unlocking the Jury Box," *Policy Review*, May/June 1996.

Walter Berns

"Getting Away with Murder," *Commentary*, April 1994.

Alexander Cockburn

"An Insult to Clarence Darrow," *Nation*, November 27, 1995.

Tanya E. Coke

"Lady Justice May Be Blind, but Is She a Soul Sister? Race-Neutrality and the Ideal of Representative Juries," *New York University Law Review*, May 1994.

Mark Curriden

"Jury Reform," *ABA Journal*, November 1995.

Maura Dolan and
Josh Meyer

"Judging the Jury System," *Los Angeles Times*, September 25–28, 1994. Available from Reprints Department, Times Mirror Square, Los Angeles, CA 90053.

Sophfronia Scott
Gregory

"Oprah! Oprah in the Court!" *Time*, June 6, 1994.

Benjamin Holden,
Laurie P. Cohen,
and Elena de Lisser

"Color Blinded: Race Seems to Play an Increasing Role in Many Jury Verdicts," *Wall Street Journal*, October 5, 1995.

Kenneth Jost

"The Jury System," *CQ Researcher*, November 10, 1995. Available from 1414 22nd St. NW, Washington, DC 20037.

Wade Lambert

"The Business of Law: Lawyers and Clients: Jury Consultants Lose Mystique as Firms Tighten Their Belts," *Wall Street Journal*, February 4, 1994.

Michael Lind

"Jury Dismissed: The Institution from the Dark Ages," *New Republic*, October 23, 1995.

Seth Lubove

"Who's on Trial?" *Forbes*, March 25, 1996.

New York Times

"Guilty or Not Guilty, 10 to 2?" September 1, 1995.

New York Times

"A Jury System for Jurors," October 27, 1994.

Henry Reske

"Generation X Jurors a Challenge," *ABA Journal*, October 1995.

Julie Shoop

"After O.J.: Panel Looks at Race and the Jury," *Trial*, December 1995.

Amy Singer

"Selecting Jurors: What to Do About Bias," *Trial*, April 1996.

Mary B.W. Tabor

"Stereotyping Men, Women, and Juries by Trial and Error," *New York Times*, February 6, 1994.

James Q. Wilson

"Reading Jurors' Minds," *Commentary*, February 1996.

Index

ABA Journal, 13, 18
Abramson, Jeffrey, 28
Adler, Stephen J., 10, 13, 14
African Americans, 23, 42-43, 45, 46, 47
  as jurors, 11, 64-67, 69, 70-71, 73
  see also discrimination; imprisonment; jury nullification
Agacinski, Bob, 71, 72
Alschuler, Albert, 12, 14, 40
American Bar Association (ABA), 12, 14, 17
American Criminal Law Review, 41, 49
American Jury, The (Kalven and Zeisel), 29, 30, 33
Andersen, Hans Christian, 42, 44, 46, 49
Apodaca v. Oregon, 25, 28, 30, 31, 33
Arizona Supreme Court, 16, 18
Australia, 25

Babcock, Barbara Allen, 22
Baltimore, Md., 68
Barry, Marion, 63-64, 70
Batson v. Kentucky, 40, 44, 45, 46, 50
  and race-based peremptory challenges, 13, 42
Beckman, M.J. "Red," 57
Blackmun, Harry, 44, 45
Bobbitt, Lorena, 11
Boyd, Walter Charles, 9, 10
Branch Davidians, 37, 53
Brazil, 35
Brooks, Kareem, 9
Brown, Raymond, 41
Burger, Warren, 48
Butler, Paul, 63, 70, 71

California, 15
California District Attorneys Association, 13, 14, 18, 72
Charen, Mona, 70
civil disobedience, 60
Civil War, American, 55
Clark, Marcia, 71
CNN, 71
cocaine, 9
Columbia Law School, 11
Crown Heights (Brooklyn, N.Y.) riot, 69-70

Dains, David, 52, 53

Dann, B. Michael, 15, 16, 17
Darryl Smith case, 72
Davies, Christie, 19
defense lawyers, 13, 14-15, 17, 42, 45, 72
Denny, Reginald, 59
Dershowitz, Alan M., 11, 17
Detroit, Mich., 71, 72, 73
DiGenova, Joseph, 73
DiIulio, John, 73
discrimination, 13, 64, 65, 66, 70, 71
  and peremptory challenges, 38-39, 48, 49
  and stereotypes, 47
  see also African Americans
Dodge, Larry, 51, 57
Doig, Don, 57,
Douglas, William, 31, 33
DuBois, W.E.B., 42, 49
Dupre, Leigh, 71, 72

England, 15, 25, 32, 55
  and history of jury nullification, 54
  jury selection in, 12
Evans, Edward, 68

Founding Fathers, of USA, 54, 55
Fugitive Slave Act, 61, 65
Fully Informed Jury Association (FIJA), 57, 58

Georgia v. McCollum, 45
Glen Ridge, N.J., rape case, 36-37
Gossage, Donald, 72
Grace, Bobby, 71
Grotewold, Garry, 52, 53

Hans, Valerie, 11, 14-15
Harper's Magazine, 70
Harvey, Bruce, 13
Hastie, Reid, 31, 32
Hayek, Friedrich, 61, 62
Heaney, Lois, 10
Hisim, Ahmet, 72, 73
hung juries, 15, 23, 26, 30
  are less frequent with majority verdict, 32
  are rarely caused by solitary juror, 33
  and racism in court, 72

imprisonment
  of African Americans, 63, 64

increasing rate of, 53
wrongful, 20, 56
Ito, Lance A., 23, 24

Jacobsohn, Gary, 34
Jefferson, Thomas, 54, 55
Johnson v. Louisiana, 28, 30, 33, 35, 37
Jost, Kenneth, 9
jurors, 17
   deliberations of, 29, 35
   are rushed by majority verdict, 31,
      32, 34-35
   and mistakes, 20, 22, 23
      rarity of, 23
   and need for greater roles in trials,
      15
   and need for more information, 54,
      56, 57-58
   and need for skepticism, 10
   and pressure for unanimity, 37
   selection of, 19, 20, 38-39, 40, 60
   public discontent with, 13-14
   should swap roles with judges, 21
   see also majority verdict; peremptory
      challenges; unanimous verdict
jury nullification
   definition of, 53-54
   history of, 53-56, 61, 65-66
   should be described to jurors, 51-58
      because some convictions are
         unjust, 51-52
      to protect constitutional freedom,
         53-56
   racially based,
      can create justice, 63-67
      injustice of, 68-73
   should not be allowed, 59-61

jury system, 9-17
   as American institution, 22, 24, 35
   changes in, 10-11
   in Europe/U.S., 10, 12
   history of, 14, 26
   should be abolished, 19-21
   should be retained, 22-24, 34
   see also jurors; jury nullification
Kalven, Harry, Jr., 29, 30, 33, 35, 36,
   37
Kennedy, Anthony, 44
King, Nancy, 13

Langbein, John, 10
Latino Americans, 45, 48
Los Angeles, Calif., 12
Louisiana, 14, 15
Lynch, Gerard, 11, 17

Madison, James, 25
majority verdict, 14-15, 31

should be adopted, 25-27
   see also unanimous verdict
Marshall, Thurgood, 44, 47, 48
Massachusetts, 31, 32
McNeil, Velma, 68
Menendez case, 11, 23, 37, 59
militia movement, 59
minorities. *See* African Americans;
   discrimination; peremptory
   challenges
Montana Libertarian Party, 57
Munsterman, G. Thomas, 38

National Association of Criminal
   Defense, 14
National Jury Project, 10
Neverdon, Davon, 69
New Jersey, 45, 46, 47
   supreme court of, 41
New York Times, 37

O'Connor, Sandra Day, 48
O.J. Simpson case, 9, 10, 11, 15, 59
   mistreatment of jury in, 23-24
   verdict in, 14, 22, 70, 71, 73
Oregon, 14, 15, 30
   majority verdict in, 25, 31, 32

Paine, Thomas, 54
Pennyover v. Neff, 46
peremptory challenges, 12-14
   expense of, 39
   should be abolished, 38-40
   should be retained, 41-49
      to protect defendant rights, 44, 45,
         49
      to protect minorities, 42-43, 46-47,
         49
Philadelphia Inquirer, 37
Powell, Lewis, 34, 44
Powers v. Ohio, 40, 49
Prohibition, 56
prosecution lawyers, 15, 42, 63, 64, 71
Public Safety Protection Act of 1996,
   14
Pulliam, Mark S., 59
Purkett V. Elem, 13

racism. *See* discrimination
Ramirez, Deborah, 46
Rehnquist, William, 48
Revolutionary War, 65
Rodney King case, 23, 41, 48, 49
   repercussions of, 12, 19

Saks, Michael, 31
Salem witch trials, 54
Sarokin, H. Lee, 38
Scalia, Antonin, 44, 45, 48

Semel, Elizabeth, 13, 14, 17
Shaw v. Reno, 44
Shelby, Richard, 68
Simpson, O.J. *See O.J. Simpson* case
slavery, 55, 66
Smith, Darryl, 72
Span case, 51-53, 54
Sparf and Hansen v. U.S., 54, 55, 56, 57
special-interest laws, 56
Spellbring, William B., 10
Spooner, Lysander, 56-57, 59, 60
Stewart, Potter, 34

Tanzer, Jacob, 25
Thomas, Clarence, 44
Thoreau, Henry David, 60
Thurmond, Strom, 44
Totten, Greg, 13, 14, 15
Trial by Jury (Spooner), 56
trial lawyers, 12, 13, 38, 41, 48
Twain, Mark, 11, 17
Twelve Angry Men (movie), 33

unanimous verdict
  as political issue, 32
  popularity of, 33
  problems with, 26-27
  should be retained, 28-35
    for thorough jury deliberation, 31,
      32, 34-35
  see also hung juries; majority verdict
United States, 10, 12, 29, 53, 66
  Bureau of Justice Statistics, 72

changing culture of, 43-44
Congress, 25
Constitution, 46, 54, 55
rate of incarceration in, 53
Supreme Court, 13, 14, 43, 45
  is seldom unanimous, 27
  on jury nullification, 54, 55, 56, 65
  on peremptory challenges, 38, 42,
    44
  on unanimous verdict tradition,
    28-32
  and systemic discrimination, 71
University of Chicago Law School, 12,
  26
  Jury Project, 29
USA Today/CNN/Gallup poll, 65

Van Dyke, Jon, 32, 36

Wall Street Journal, 10
Washington, D.C., 9, 23
Washington Post, 17, 68
Weaver, Randy, 53
Weiss, Michael, 68
Whitehead, G. Marc, 12, 14, 17
Wilson, Pete, 15
women, 48

Yale Law Journal, 70
Yale Law School, 10

Zeisel, Hans, 29, 30, 33, 35, 36, 37
Zinsmeister, Karl, 68